H R ole Kulet's Blossoms of the Savannah: A Complete Guide

A Guide Book to H R ole Kulet's Blossoms of the Savannah, Volume 4

Jorges P. Lopez

Published by Jorges P. Lopez, 2023.

H R OLE KULET'S BLOSSOMS OF THE SAVANNAH: A COMPLETE GUIDE

First edition. December 14, 2023.

ISBN: 979-8223626633

Written by Jorges P. Lopez.

Also by Jorges P. Lopez

A Guide Book to H R ole Kulet's Blossoms of the Savannah
H R ole Kulet's Blossoms of the Savannah: Plot Analysis and Characters
H R ole Kulet's Blossoms of the Savannah: Themes and Elements of Style
H R ole Kulet's Blossoms of the Savannah: Answering Excerpt & Essay Questions
H R ole Kulet's Blossoms of the Savannah: A Complete Guide

A Guide Book to Margaret A Ogola's The River and the Source
The River and the Source: Plot Analysis and Characters
The River and the Source: Themes and Elements of Style
Margaret Ogola The River and the Source: Answering Excerpt & Essay Questions
Margaret Ogola The River and the Source: A Complete Guide

A Guide to Bertolt Brecht's The Caucasian Chalk Circle
The Caucasian Chalk Circle: Plot Analysis and Characters
The Caucasian Chalk Circle: Themes and Elements of Style

Bertolt Brecht's The Caucasian Chalk Circle: Dealing with Excerpts & Essay Questions

Bertolt Brecht The Caucasian Chalk Circle: A Complete Guide

A Guide to Henrik Ibsen's A Doll's House

Henrik Ibsen's A Doll's House: Plot Analysis and Characters

Henrik Ibseb's A Doll's House: Themes and Elements of Style

Henrik Ibsen's A Dolls House: Answering Excerpt & Essay Questions

A Guide to Kazuo Ishiguro's An Artist of the Floating World

An Artist of the Floating World: Plot Analysis and Characters

An Artist of the Floating World: Themes and Elements of Style

Kazuo Ishiguro's An Artist of the Floating World: Answering Excerpt & Essay Questions

A Guide to Reading A Silent Song and Other Stories ed. by Godwin Siundu

A Silent Song and Other Stories Edited by Godwin Siundu : Volume One

A Silent Song and Other Stories edited by Godwin Siundu : Volume Two

A Silent Song and Other Stories edited by Godwin Siundu : Volume Three

A Guide to Reading John Lara's The Samaritan

Reading John Lara's The Samaritan: Plot Analysis and Characters

John Lara's The Samaritan: Themes and Elements of Style
John Lara's The Samaritan: Answering Excerpt and Essay Questions

A Study Guide to Paul B. Vitta's Fathers of Nations

Paul B. Vitta's Fathers of Nations: Plot Analysis and Characters
Paul B. Vitta's Fathers of Nations: Themes and Elements of Style
Paul B Vitta's Fathers of Nations: Answering excerpt & Essay Questions

Essay Writing

Writing the Grade A Essay

JIMMY DIARIES SERIES

Jimmy Karda
Jimmy and his Ancestor
Jimmy and the Ramshackle
Jimmy and the Covid 19 Scare

Poetry

Silent Musings : Poetry
Silent Musings: Poetry

Reading John Steinbeck's The Pearl

John Steinbeck's The Pearl: Plot Analysis and Characters
John Steinbeck's The Pearl: Themes and Elements of Style

John Steinbeck's The Pearl: Answering Excerpt and Essay Questions
John Steinbeck's The Pearl: A Complete Guide

Short Stories

Beauty's in a Mark

To Be a Groom

St. Maryan Seven Series

Amy

St. Maryan Seven The Westgate Rescue

St. Maryan Seven and the Dubai Allure

For Purity

READING H.R. Ole Kulet's Blossoms of the Savannah

First Printing Nairobi, 2018

Jorges P. Lopez

Introduction

- **This book focuses on the KENYA CERTIFICATE OF SECONDARY EDUCATION English Papers 101/2 – in which candidates answer questions based on an EXCERPT taken from a specific set text studied during the course to earn 25 marks – and 101/3 – in which candidates answer 3 questions (each with 20 marks) in two and a half hours. The skills taught here, however, are applicable to any examination. The only thing required is to examine the time and marks given in your own exam and make appropriate adjustments. Some College exams, for instance, require the student to answer a question in ONE HOUR to earn 25 marks. The candidate should adjust the time suggested here and paragraphing to fit this particular exam.**

Following its predecessors, *Reading Margaret Ogola's* The River and the Source, *Reading Bertolt Brecht's* The Caucasian Chalk Circle, *Reading John Steinbeck's* The Pearl and *Reading Henrik Ibsen's* A Doll's House, this book embraces the design of that quartet. It shows you how to deal with *Blossoms of the Savannah* through comprehension questions to arrive at an understanding that allows you to communicate with both Ole Kulet and his critics or critics of similar texts. This advances from the researched, tried and proven theory that literature students underachieve because their approach to literary texts and their presentation of answers is wanting; a student has to know a text fully to discuss it and present personal opinions. To do so, one needs to read the text and consult other critics to form a balanced opinion. Similarly, many students study thoroughly but still fail to do well because their presentation of ideas is inadequate.

This guide book lets you discern the elements of literature – plot, theme, character and style – on your own. It helps you understand *Blossoms of the Savannah* so as to grasp the plot, infer themes, characters and style without necessarily consulting a teacher. To do so, follow the questions at the end of every section and answer them truthfully. Where this is difficult, go back to the particular section and reread it keenly before continuing.

This text contains a series of twelve questions after every section. The first set of four questions helps you identify **important facts** from what is read. The next set helps you **interpret these facts** in order to see their significance. This should help you see the connectedness of the plot and also understand characters thus making the novelist's intention clearer. The last set of questions helps you apply - label - what is interpreted, that is, see what has been interpreted in terms of themes, character traits or elements of style because, after all, this is the point of studying any literature text. This is what an examiner will ask.

To do this, it is important to understand that the **first** question should lead to the **fifth** and the fifth to the **ninth**. The **second** should lead to the **sixth** and the sixth to the **tenth** and so on. By the time all the questions have been answered, the elements of literature you are meant to derive from this text should become obvious. For the teacher using this text, these sets of questions help you test the student's understanding of the plot before proceeding to a detailed analysis. The second and third set of questions indeed help the student in this analysis so that by the time the student is through with the plot, all that is required is a collation of the elements already discovered. This should help the student in debating themes, character traits and elements of style discussed after the plot analysis of the book.

This book also contains a detailed guide on how to go about **context** and **essay** questions and how to **interpret**, **plan** and **write** down your answers with a view to *earning all the marks* given for every question. This should help the student to see how many marks have been earned and where marks have been lost in an exam situation. It is encouraged that the student and the teacher do this practically in class because it helps the student to think like an examiner.

The Author

A prolific writer of fiction, Henry Rupes ole Kulet has enjoyed a wide writing career spanning close to fifty years. Born in 1946 at Enkare Ngusur village, he attended Siyiapei Primary school and later went to Kilgoris for his Upper Primary education before proceeding to Narok High School. It was here that he discovered his writing talent after an article he wrote – which was inspired by President Jomo Kenyatta's visit to their school – caught attention after being published in a major newspaper. He studied for a diploma in personnel management before being employed by the Kenya farmers Association.,

Ole kulet has been a champion of both Maasai culture and environment capturing their cultural and historical experiences. Each successive novel reveals some intricacy of Maasai culture. His characters exhibit existential problems to do with the cultural clash between the old and the new. They show the attempt to live and be relevant in a changing society, especially because the Maasai have been able to largely stick to their culture and traditions in the face of debilitating colonialism and westernization. Many of his novels have also used the girl child as an agent of change in an emerging society. Ole Kulet first arrived on the literary scene in 1971 with the publication of *Is it Possible*? He was then twenty-five years old. He followed this with *To Become a Man* in 1972, *The Hunter* (1985), *Daughter of Maa* (1987), *Moran No More* (1990) *Bandits of Kibi* (1999) and *Blossoms of the Savannah* (2009).

His novels have been read and studied near and far. *Is it Possible* and *To Become a Man* have been set books in East Africa. The two novels have also been translated into French, German and Swedish. His novel *Vanishing Herds* won the 2013 Jomo Kenyatta Prize for Literature following in the footsteps of *Blossoms of the Savannah* which had won the same prize in 2009.

The Text

Blossoms of the Savannah which won the 2009 Jomo Kenyatta Prize for Literature is a classic Ole Kulet novel. While keeping true to Maasai setting and characterization, the novel focuses on the issue of Female Genital Cutting often referred to as Female Genital Mutilation or FGM. Its peculiarity is the fact that this topic has been associated with female writers especially western feminists. The novel tackles this sensitive topic against the background of teenage rebellion, parental and patriarchal authority as well as material greed. Parsimei Ole Kaelo finds himself compelled to move to the countryside to start a business after being retrenched. He falls prey to Oloisudori Loonkiyaa, a ruthless business tycoon well known for his extortionist tendencies. This time however, Oloisudori wants payback in form of Resian, one of Ole Kaelo's daughters. This daughter must be prepared for him by going though circumcision so as to become a fitting, socially accepted wife for Oloisudori.

However, the father and the businessman get a lot more than they bargain for. Resian runs away from home to avoid both the marriage and the forced cut. Aided by unlikely people, she ends up at the farm of Minik ene Nkoitoi, a hated feminist who runs a rescue home for girls running away from forced marriage and forced circumcision. When

Oloisudori comes in hot pursuit of either Resian or her sister – who is also rescued by Minik's agents after being forcefully circumcised – he faces up to the uncompromising Minik. His stubbornness leads to the loss of his gleaming fleet of limousines which goes up in smoke and he and his cohorts have to flee. Resian and her sister finally join Egerton University which has been their shared ambition from the very start.

The Synopsis of the Plot

Chapter 1 – Meet the Kaelos, and their Troubles

The narrative opens in the bedroom of Kaelo's two daughters. Early morning, from the window of their room in the heart of Nakuru town, Taiyo watches her father directing the loading of the family property on to vehicles that will move the family to their new home in Nasila. She recalls her father's aggressively hostile attitude as she recollects his denying her permission to visit Mombasa on a music tour. Resian joins her at the window and the two poignantly ponder over leaving Nakuru. We learn that Ole Kaelo was recently retrenched and that he has built a shop in Nasila. Taiyo is especially sad at leaving her boyfriend. The two girls are apprehensive at the prospects in Nasila but Taiyo is optimistic her father's business will succeed. Resian expresses her wish to study veterinary medicine at Egerton University and become a doctor. She asks her sister to broach this subject with their father but Taiyo is non-committal.

Their mother calls them to help with the parking but it is the sight of their father coming that moves them. The family soon leaves for Nasila. In the vehicle, different thoughts stream through each one's mind. Mama Milanoi is appreciative of her marriage but anxious about how her daughters will be received at Nasila. Ole Kaelo looks back at his job, his daughters and the future. He is close to Taiyo but detests Resian who has blossomed into a woman already and who he'd want to marry off quickly. They soon arrive in Nasila and are welcomed by his brother's family.

Chapter 2 – New home, Dad visits Supeyo

The following morning, Taiyo and Resian wake up to a serene atmosphere which contrasts the hustle and bustle of Nakuru. Resian thinks it is a good place to come home to from college. At breakfast they are introduced by their eldest aunt to the rest of her family; three co-wives and sixteen children. The two take a walk during which they review their relatives; Taiyo is guarded but Resian is openly critical. They are accosted by a young man who contemptuously talks of their being uncircumcised. Though they are unharmed, the girls are visibly shaken but fearing their father's reaction decide to keep the incident under wraps.

Having settled, Ole Kaelo visits his friend Ole Supeyo, a wealthy businessman who trusts him but though comfortably living with some changes, is vehemently opposed to Nkoitoi's crusade against FGM. Kaelo is welcomed by Supeyo and the two talk business. Kaelo reveals he's made inroads in contracts and Supeyo tries to advise the younger man; he is surprised when he hears that Kaelo has banked on Oloisudori for his business progress. He advises Kaelo to be cautious especially with his daughters. That afternoon, the Kaelos go to their new home. While his wife and daughters run excitedly to the new house, Kaelo is left behind nervous at Supeyo's reaction to his trust in Oloisudori.

Chapter 3 – Settling Down, Neighbors' aspirations

As they approach their new house, Mama Milanoi reflects on her relationship with her husband. She married him according to tradition and to her, he is a diligent, responsible man though she feels she has disappointed him for not giving him a son. She also feels powerless to help her daughters in the impending social conflict. Ole Kaelo ushers his family into their new home which stuns all. The family goes about settling. The girls review cultural traditions of Nasila and their position regarding them. Resian is vehement about her resistance to tradition and resorts to her sister's protection. Taiyo thinks of her protection of Resian through the years – from bullies, a hateful father and an ignorant mother. The girls begin acclimatizing to their new setting – and to Nasila culture; they have no privacy and have to cook and serve many people who visit without notice. They settle down, even beginning to enjoy the new environment especially now since their father is often away at the shop. Many women visit to judge the girls' suitability as co-wives or wives for their sons. Midwifes and circumcisers come to gauge potential clients. One day, their father announces his intention to hold a homecoming ceremony.

Commentary

We are immediately struck by Ole Kaelo's temper and his daughters' apprehension in and out of his presence. Mama Milanoi is docile while Taiyo tolerates her father but Resian has grown rebellious. Ole Kaelo regrets not having sons especially blaming his second daughter. He is detached from his larger family and clan and has let his younger brother run the family's affairs. In chapter 2, the serene countryside contrasts Nakuru town. Kaelo's daughters directly encounter what's awaiting in the countryside as they are accosted by a young man. Kaelo on the other hand has a rude shock when he finds out that he has put his trust on a very dangerous man. The conflict in the family deters Kaelo's daughters from being open to their parents about their encounter.

Ole Kaelo's business dream turns gloomy when he learns about Oloisudori's cunning. As his family settles down, he is uneasy about what the future might hold. His daughters are similarly apprehensive about their reception in Nasila, especially because of their uncircumcised status. They must also get used to the fact that in Nasila, the community is one large extension of the family.

Question for Plot Comprehension

Identifying Important Facts

1. One of the biggest **conflicts** in this narrative is **generational**. How is the stage set for this conflict in the Kaelo family? How does Kaelo relate with each of his daughters? Why is this important in the wider social conflict of the novel?
2. What's the image of Ole Kaelo in chapter1? How does he relate with his workers? What **image** do you get of his focus – his retirement and the destiny of his family?
3. The theme of Family is important in this novel. How is it introduced in the birth of Kaelo's children? How do the parents react and what does this show about their society?
4. Explain what is **foreshadowed** by Resian's wish to become a doctor. How is this central to the suspense in the narrative?

Interpreting Facts for Meaning

1. How is the conflict in the Kaelo family developed in chapter 2? How important is the girls' keeping the attack on them a secret and Kaelo not confiding what he learns at Ole Supeyo's with his family?
2. How is the formidable picture of Kaelo shattered when he visits Ole Supeyo? In how many ways is his self-**assurance** broken as seen on his way home from Supeyo's place?
3. How is Kaelo and Milanoi's treatment of their children central to their daughters' characters? Examine how far each daughter's development is a reaction to the parents' attitude.

4. Where else in chapter 2 does Resian talk about her **ambition**? Is in what way is this ambition more manifest here? Why is the movement to Nasila ironic considering this? What are Taiyo's ambitions?

Applying meanings

1. How do Mama Milanoi's reflections give meaning and basis to the conflict in her family? What is her role in the father/ daughter conflict between Ole Kaelo and Resian? How does this make Taiyo grow up before her time?
2. How far has Ole Kaelo's character changed since we met him? What do we learn of his character from his wife and Taiyo's reflections? Use **adjectives** to qualify his character so far.
3. How is Ole Kaelo responsible for Resian's **rebellious** attitude? Do you think Ole Kaelo ought to separate family, community and clan? How is his commitment to community and clan a **betrayal** of his family?
4. Why do you think the author finds it necessary to introduce Taiyo as Resian's protector here? How far do Taiyo's reminisces here illuminate the characters of her sister and her father?

Chapter 4 – Homecoming, Taiyo meets Parmuat

Ole Kaelo holds his homecoming ceremony. Through him, we learn that many traditions are stereotypical. The ceremony is showy with a lot of food and young clansmen being paid to ensure it is a success. We note Ole Kaelo's effect on his daughter when he meets Resian in the house; she is so nervous she breaks glasses. There is a lot of eating and dancing at the house with school children conducted by Joseph Parmuat who we learn, Taiyo has fallen in love with, singing Ole Kaelo's praises. It turns out that Parmuat is a clansman of Taiyo hence intimate relations are taboo. Taiyo takes pity on and feeds one old man who turns out to be Ole Musanka, the main speaker/elder of the occasion. He welcomes Ole Kaelo back to the clan warning him it is his duty to reattach himself to his community. As an after-thought, he warns the girls against listening to Minik ene Nkoitoi about girl circumcision. He curses Minik and specially praises Taiyo for feeding him and prophesies that she'll be the mother of the next leader of Nasila and the Maa. This gladly pleases Ole Kaelo but the girls and their mother are troubled by especially the reference to Minik.

Chapter 5 – Parmuat's Coaching, The Flashy Shop

On the evening of the ceremony marking Ole Kaelo's grand return to his community, his daughters are too troubled to sleep. Taiyo is angry since culture doesn't allow any heterosexual relationship with Parmuat – but glad for her mother consents to his visits; there's a possibility of being coached in music by him – which awaits her father's consent. Resian is deeply troubled by the prospect of circumcision now made so real by Ole Musanka, especially when she remembers the vigor and energy the circumciser had shown the two girls on a previous visit to their home. She spends a sleepless night, worried about the possibility of abduction by the young man who had accosted them earlier and who had grinned at them at their father's homecoming party.

When, Ole Kaelo suggest the girls need be prepared for Nasila culture and she suggests they put family first, he goads her into acceptance of his verdict. Worried, she puts her last hope on Minik. She wonders what her daughters know about FGM. Ole Kaelo has another clash with Resian which sours their bond further. Later, the family visits Ole Kaelo's shop. Resian is critical of the display of wealth and hopes her father won't claim he has no money when asked about going to the university. Taiyo is however appreciative of the shop and Resian is forced to agree with her. Joseph Parmuat visits the three ladies that evening but his welcome visit is spoiled by the arrival of a silent, uninvited Olarinkoi who has to be accommodated as communal hospitality demands.

Chapter 6 – Parmuat's Coaching, Yeiyo-botorr, Olarinkoi

Ole Kaelo arrives to find the seated family but the girls withdraw only to be recalled. He gives an evasive speech but finally impresses the girls on the need to embrace their culture to protect their family; 'It should never happen to us,' 71. Their mother later emphasizes his speech but the girls wear blank faces. Taiyo's coaching by Parmuat is allowed; she is ecstatic. Resian is dismissive of their father's leading them '...back to the stone-age era' but Taiyo mollifies her anger. As they sleep, Resian voices her disquiet about their father's getting them a man and not a woman to 'teach them culture' seeing the position of the woman as disadvantaged in this society. Taiyo dismisses her fears.

The following afternoon, Parmuat visits them again – and so does Olarinkoi, who makes his visits habitual afterwards. Parmuat doesn't see eye to eye with him although he butts in to give his opinions on the things Parmuat teaches the girls. The following day, the girls aunt, yeiyo-botorr, visits and joins them in cooking. She praises the girls on their 'woman' skills in cooking but Resian takes issue with this claiming men should also cook. This shocks the three other women with her mother asking her what is wrong with her. Resian stands her ground which angers her aunt and she leaves claiming that Resian's attitude is caused by a bad spirit because she is uncircumcised. Resian's mother and sister are surprised and her mother wonders whether she should inform her husband; she is sure he would call for the circumciser the following day.

Taiyo, disturbed by the secretive Olarinkoi asks Parmuat for an explanation - Parmuat gives her two versions of stories about Olarinkoi. The first emphasizes the mystery of the real man while the second traces the origin of FGM. He ends the story by stating that women started the practice and only they can end it.

Chapter 7 – Milanoi broaches FGM, Oloisudori Visits

Taiyo leaves with her father and Resian hopes she will get a chance to broach the subject of going to university within the day. Mama Milanoi broaches the subject of FGM with Resian who informs her she already knows about the origin of FGM from despotic Olarinkoi but argues that modern men are the Olarinkoi because they are the ones who continue to perpetuate the practice of FGM. The discussion is rudely interrupted by the entry of Oloisudori who comes looking for Ole Kaelo, inviting himself to the house and refusing to leave despite Resian's anger at him. Ole Kaelo is thoroughly scared when he arrives home to find Oloisudori. He sweats and speaks with a tremor in his voice Resian flees behind the house where she finds her sister and Parmuat. Parmuat explains the nature of Oloisudori to them. We learn that the man is a thief, a smuggler and an extortionist. The girls are aghast. Taiyo informs her sister that she was unable to fulfil her promise of asking their father about the university. Resian on the other hand informs her about their mother's broaching the subject of FGM and her frank opinion about it.

Their father returns and orders Resian to the kitchen. Taiyo asks her father about his relationship with Oloisudori but he is cagey. In spite of his obvious nervousness, he assures her that he is in control. The girls are surprised by their mother's similar nervousness which makes her burn the rice for supper.

Commentary

The family conflict deepens with Ole Kaelo's homecoming ceremony which effectively rejoins him to his clan and his people. The ceremony is symbolic of his acceptance by the people and it also pushes the conflict further for the question of the girls' reintegration into the community through circumcision is openly broached. Taiyo's character is stressed in foreshadowing her as the mother of the next Maa leader making the future direction of the community symbolic. The arrival of the girls' aunt in chapter 5 stresses the course they are expected to follow; circumcision is thus conclusive and the girls' opinion is not required. Resian liberal dissent further plunges the family into deeper conflict while the arrival of Parmuat to 'teach' the girls openly states Ole Kaelo's intention. Her criticism of her father's flashiness and the stress on university education creates deeper foreboding. Chapter six well prepares the girls for rebellion by showing that women are solely responsible for their exploitation. Parmuat's narrative symbolically shows that women have led themselves into the trap of FGM and are therefore solely responsible for its ending.

Oloisudori's arrival presents a new angle. His intolerable nature suggests Ole Kaelo is forced to deal with him. His utter fear and intimidation casts a shadow on the business dealings between the two men. He is however cagey while his wife is taciturn. Both remain mum about the turn of events occasioning Oloisudori's visit and the state of affairs his visit leaves the family in.

Identifying Important facts

1. **Circumcision** has so far remained just a threat to the Ole Kaelo daughters. Where in chapter four does it become a forgone conclusion? How does each of the girls reaction to this?
2. Before now, Resian's **dissenting** attitude has only been directed at her sister. Pick several examples in the previous chapters to prove this.
3. **Feminism** is a major theme in the novel. What problems are identified in chapters 4 & 5 as preventing **woman's**

determinism? What is the older generation's attitude to this?

4. **Imagery** and **foreshadowing** play a big role in narrative development in these four chapters. What role does Ole Musanka's praise of Taiyo and reference to *Emakererei* play in forecasting the narrative? How does it heighten the **conflict**?

Interpreting Facts for Meaning

1. How is the conclusion in chapter four stressed by the arrival of Olarinkoi, and ironically, by the visit of Parmuat? Do you think Olarinkoi's visit is arranged by Ole Kaelo? Give reasons. Why do you think Olarinkoi offers uncalled for **opinions**?
2. How does Resian's **criticism** grow to include the wider society in chapter five? What two previous incidents lead her into this boldness? Use **adjectives** to capture her emerging character.
3. How does Resian represent the **determination of the new woman**? How does her age and **intelligence** contrast that of the older women? What is the author's point?
4. What **images** are drawn of Olarinkoi and Oloisudori? What do their names suggest and how do they forecast their characters in particular and the narrative in general?

Applying Meanings

1. What role does Yeiyo-botorr play in *furthering* the **conflict**? How does Parmuat's narrative crown this conflict to intensify *complications*? How is the old Olarinkoi **symbolized** by the modern Olarinkoi in the narrative? How is Oloisudori a **symbolized** modern Olarinkoi? What do you think Oloisudori visits the family about? How can we tell?
2. Resian's character development continues in chapters 6 & 7. Look for **adjectives** to describe her in her **boldness** to Yeiyo-botorr and her intelligent interpretation of modern

Olarinkoi. What is her conclusion about the history of the plight of women? Do you agree with her?

3. In chapters 6 & 7, Ole Kulet shows that women liberation requires guts. How is this shown through;

   i. Resian's intelligence
   ii. Resian's bold confrontation of modern fallacies?
   iii. Contrast between the young and the old?

1. What **image** are we given of Ole Kaelo upon his finding Oloisudori in his house? How does this emphasize the image of Oloisudori already created by his entry, his behavior towards Resian and her fear for him? What point do you think Ole Kulet tries to drive home?

Chapter 8 – Sleepless Nights, Guilt and a Little Relenting

The Kaelo couple spend a sleepless night. Kaelo rues meeting Oloisudori; he is forced to reconcile with his own greed which led him to Oloisudori and to accept Oloisudori's rotten business practices. Kaelo remembers Oloisudori's visit and the latter's open avowal that he wanted to marry Resian while a friend of his was interested in Taiyo. He silently agonizes, reflecting on his daughters' growing up and his love for them, now that he finds himself forced to marry them off to men they do not choose. Mama Milanoi agonizes in her own way. She reflects on her husband's exposé of the source of their wealth and the prospect of marrying her daughter off to a son-in-law the age of her husband. She worries over her powerlessness remembering her youth when women would have a plan of action in such situations. She reflects on the cultural erosion that leaves people like her at the mercy of those of Oloisudori's ilk. The couple discusses how to go about breaking the news of marriage to Resian but Mama Milanoi urges caution arguing that there's still time.

The following morning Ole Kaelo is unusually cheerful and Resian is alarmed at his artificiality. Ironically, Taiyo is glad thinking that her father's sense of strength is necessary for the family. Their mother is similarly cheerful and the Kaelo's are a happy family at breakfast. Kaelo consents to Parmuat coaching his daughters in music and dance and his enthusiasm almost makes Resian put in her request about joining the university. She however thinks that if rejected, it would be difficult to bring it up again; she opts for patience. Olarinkoi joins them at breakfast and ironically Resian fetches him a cup for tea. Mama Milanoi is hurt knowing the pointlessness of all the cheer.

Chapter 9 – Parmuat's Cultural Lessons, Taiyo Falls in Love

Joseph Parmuat begins coaching the girls but while Taiyo is enthralled, Resian is bored and soon gives up altogether. Taiyo and Parmuat find it difficult because they are obviously attracted to one another and Taiyo is sardonic of culture. Parmuat is careful to remain within the bounds of culture and not hurt Taiyo. He teaches the girls their culture especially the two types of youthful love. The three discuss the basics of culture with Resian stating that had she the power, she'd examine culture to get rid of hateful aspects. Parmuat draws out such features that have already been done away with. The girls wonder at men's scramble to marry young girls when there are many unmarried girls elsewhere such as Nakuru town. Noting that Taiyo is unreservedly drawn to him, Parmuat tries to avoid contact with her eyes but Taiyo is determined.

Taiyo visits Parmuat's house the next day but finds him out. He finds her probing his orderly house upon his return. She is ashamed and apologizes but Parmuat stops her apologies. The two openly declare their love and become passionate with Taiyo openly defying the culture that denies her the right to love Parmuat. The two resolve to love one another despite the limitations of culture with Taiyo warning for caution so as not to hurt others especially her father. Taiyo reflects on culture and the position it gives her seeing Emakererei as their saving leader and wishing she could follow in her shoes.

On his part, Parmuat is deeply troubled. He isn't sure whether loving Taiyo and forsaking his culture is a good thing even though he deeply loves her. He is torn between loving her and defying his culture; finally he resolves to forsake her love and uphold his culture.

Chapter 10 – Desperate Parents Seek Advice, Girls Attacked

Ole Kaelo and his wife become even more desperate. Unable to find a solution to their problem, Ole Kaelo resolves to visit his friend Ole Supeyo while Milanoi decides to seek help from the Simiren's wives. Resian is overly suspicious and becomes both sensitive and superstitious but Taiyo is gay and becomes the only light in the gloomy, despondent house. She always looks forward to the arrival of Parmuat. The girls visit their father's shop and on their way home are accosted again – this time by two men, one of whom is the one that accosted them on their second day in Nasila. They are rescued by Olarinkoi who beats the men and sends the girls home. The girls are grateful. At home, Resian is angry about male behavior in this society and contemplates flight. Taiyo on the other hand is further resolved in her belief that she is a combatant who should join Emakererei in fighting for women and child's rights.

Commentary

Things come to a head and Kaelo has to pay for his shortsightedness. Oloisudori bluntly tries to wrest his daughters from him as if they were objects in a market. Kaelo's sense of inevitability is ironic since his closed mind does not see any option other than marrying off his daughters despite his living in modern times, suggesting that his withdrawal to Nasila is premeditated.

Apparently, it is shown that women's power has been eroded with time. In the past, women could report such matters to elders or even take mass action. The Kaelos remain hypocritical to the recent happenings with the parents remaining mum about the marriage and circumcision arrangements. Taiyo is lost in the bliss of being allowed to practice music and dance while Resian bids her time to get a chance to demand to be allowed to join Egerton University.

Positive elements of culture are shown in types of youthful love and checks and balances that culture uses to keep the youth disciplined and in check. Similarly, it gives measures for penalty of erring persons. Taiyo sees Minik's leadership as crucial in changing such things. She also sees herself as part of that change. Ole Kulet is critical of cultural traits that leave the youth in limbo; Parmuat is as passionate about his culture and what it does to his society as he is about Taiyo. Ole Kulet shows that men are more stoic about such matters when Parmuat chooses his culture over his girlfriend. A philosophical statement is therefore made later when he dies while Taiyo survives.

Chapter 10 sees the girls resolve in hating Nasila culture go rise. Their being rudely waylaid leads them to believe they don't belong to this society. Interestingly, it is the detested, ever present, ever quiet Olarinkoi who rescues them leaving the reader feeling he is forever after the girls like their shadow.

Identifying Important Facts

1. What would you say is the **central conflict** in chapter 8? Is it more of **external** or **internal**? What feelings go through each of the characters and how does this affect their relationship with one another?
2. How does Ole Kulet bring out **parental hypocrisy** through Milanoi and Kaelo in chapter 8? What do you think they should do for their children in the face of people like

Oloisudori in their society?

3. In what way does Ole Kulet show that **women's power** has greatly been lost through time? How is this shown by the relationship between Milanoi and Ole Kaelo?
4. What **image** is cut by the narrative Mama Milanoi remembers of her youth? What is **symbolized** by the girl leading an old man on a *leash* and the men running to the hills? What is the **symbolism** of the men being *'allowed'* back to the village in the evening?

Interpreting Facts for meaning

1. Why do you think the author **focuses** on **youth** in chapter 9? What goals of the youth are captured especially through Taiyo and Parmuat?
2. Explain how the author draws **contrast** between **parental hypocrisy** in chapter 8 and **children's sincerity** through Taiyo and Parmuat in chapter 9. How do young people opening up to one another further this point. What does Taiyo and Parmuat's openness symbolize?
3. While Milanoi is **powerless** in chapter 8, especially pitted against her husband, Taiyo is openly more **decisive** than Parmuat. What point do you think the author makes through this? How is this emphasized later when Parmuat *dies* while Taiyo lives and *goes to university*? How is she **symbolic** of both the **woman of the future** as well as future leaders?
4. What **images** are cut by 'fishing in shallow waters' pg. 129? What is the **symbolism** of Taiyo winning over Parmuat on pg. 135? Explain the use and value of the images of war, liberation and combatants here.

Applying Meanings

1. How does the attack on the girls change their view of Nasila society? Why do you think it is Olarinkoi who is at hand to rescue them?
2. Do you think the secret mission of Ole Kaelo and his wife has any role in the attack on the girls? Might it have been planned to intimidate them? Why is it that it is Olarinkoi who saves them? What lesson does the attack teach the girls? Should the parents be accused of neglect?
3. Why do you think Ole Kulet denies the girls *physical power* to tackle their attack? What kind of power does he suggest women need? How is this emphasized by Taiyo's resolve to join Emakererei to fight for *women and children* ***rights***?
4. How is the ending of chapter ten foreshadowing? Who appears stronger between Resian and Taiyo here? Why is this ironical considering the turnout of events?

Chapter 11 – Parents Criticized, Kaelo's Revenge, Simiren Visit

The girls wait eagerly to inform their parents of the attack but the parents arrive home looking disturbed and the issue is shelved. Ole Kaelo fails in his mission to persuade Ole Supeyo to take his stocks. Milanoi's mission fails too; she and her husband are accused of bestriding two paths like the proverbial hyena. Simiren's wife challenge her to let the girls live with them for some time arguing that the girls may even ask to be circumcised of their own accord once they get used to living with the Simirens. The parents are angry when they learn of the attack on their daughters. Kaelo storms out of the house armed and Milanoi takes the chance to ask her daughters to go live with the Simirens for some time. By noon, they are dispatched to the Simirens where they are gladly welcomed. They are easily integrated into the family where they learn firsthand the positive elements of Nasila culture. They especially learn how to share and be selfless. Living with yeiyo-kiti, the girls learn many things. They learn that yeiyo-kiti was a classmate of Emakererei and express their wish to join the fearless Emakererei and change Nasila culture. As they go to draw water, the two girls are preoccupied with thoughts of Emakererei. Resian hopes to join her while Taiyo thinks of composing a song in her honor.

The girls' parents summon them home on the eve of the special day when special meals are taken at Simiren's home. Their parents come for them and Resian is apprehensive at the looks her father gives her.

Chapter 12 – Culprits Punished, Oloisudori Postpones

Kaelo informs young men of the assault on his daughters and they join him on his way to see Parmuat at the school. On learning what has happened, Parmuat dispatches boys of their clan to inform their elder brothers and fathers to meet at the Oerata plains. The meeting identifies the suspects and resolves to retaliate with brutal force. The men are soon found hiding in bushes and they take flight to two old men to whom they appeal for intervention. They are seriously beaten before calm is restored. It is discovered that one of the victims is actually related to Milanoi. They are punished with payment of fines. Mama Milanoi is especially angry with the behavior of her relative.

We learn that Oloisudori has postponed his visit to Kaelo. Though he cannot understand Oloisudori's attachment to his daughter, Ole Kaelo finds himself forced to accept the eventuality of the marriage and begins to rationalize it. The girls learn of the fines of the young men and Resian is indignant insisting that they belong to prison. The rift between Resian and her father widens and he is forced to become more amiable. Mixing with the community makes the girls more accepted, even respected.

Chapter 13 – Oloisudori Visit, Kaelo Intimidated

Oloisudori says that he is coming to see Kaelo the next day and wants Resian to serve him. Kaelo orders the resisting Resian to stay home and make food with her mother for Oloisudori. Resian is angry and runs to the garden where she stays until dark. She reflects on the culture of her people especially what they learn at her uncle's place. After complaining a lot, she gets her way and she and Taiyo are to serve the guests together. Oloisudori arrives with a showy retinue of men as if already wedding. Kaelo is so daunted and worships him. He is feted with the parents outdoing themselves. The visitors lastly leave very impressed; they agree that Resian is 'quite a catch'. Taiyo tries to find out from her father what the visit was about fearing that the visitors might take advantage of her father like Parmuat had said. She fails because Kaelo is cagey. She fails to ask him about the university too. Kaelo calls Resian and she goes eagerly thinking that it is the matter of the university which has been settled. Kaelo is unable to discuss the matter of Resian's betrothal because his daughter ambushes him first. He dismisses her and asks her to call her mother.

Commentary

The nervous state of the Kaelo family leads Kaelo to explode into fight while Milanoi 'exports' her daughters to the Simirens to be taught culture. The polygamous family creates selfless people in society and a generally egalitarian culture. It is also suggested that children should be naturally integrated into society rather than be taught the way Ole Kaelo does with Parmuat.

We learn of a number of the society's customs through the fining of the young men who accost Ole Kaelo's daughters. The girls' independence is notable; it has further been fueled by their stay at their uncle's home. A sense of calmness prevails as the girls become more integrated into the Nasila community.

Resian conflicts further with her father when she resists being made to serve Oloisudori. Culture seems is misused here because at their uncle's place, the girls learn how their culture protects girls by keeping them away from men which their father doesn't do. Oloisudori uses objects to impress the family and appears to pay dowry by giving Kaelo a briefcase with undisclosed contents. Kaelo is guilty about marrying Resian off' whenever he tries to break the news to her, he fails miserably and the matter is postponed indefinitely.

Identifying Important Facts.

1. What do you think is Ole Kaelo's **internal conflict** upon returning from Ole Supeyo? How about his wife? Why do you think the parents react so swiftly after learning of the attack on their children?
2. Why do you think both parents are **evasive** about the problem facing their daughters? Why aren't they able to teach them about their culture the way the Simiren household does? Use **adjectives** that capture Ole Kaelo and Milanoi's character here.
3. **Culture and tradition** as a theme is revealed here. What positive elements of culture are identifiable here? How does this suggest that life – rearing children – was a lot easier in the past than it is today? **Compare** and **contrast** life in the Kaelo and Simiren households.
4. How effective is the **imagery** used in the song of **the three blind mice**? Discuss the blindness of the three in the face of a changing society.

Interpreting Facts for Meaning

1. What **motive** does Ole Kaelo have for revenging the assault on his daughters? Why is he so eager to collect people for revenge when he has no regard, chiefly, for Resian? What other **aim** might he have?
2. Resian and Taiyo are slowly accepted by the community upon

return from Simiren's home. Why does this happen? What does this show about their parents' effort to integrate them into Nasila society? Who is the **alien** at the end of the chapter, the parents or the daughters?

3. What ways are in place for punishing wayward people as shown in this chapter? Why is it then that nothing can be done about Oloisudori? Who's to blame therefore, the **parents** or the **society**?
4. How is **rhetoric questioning** used on pg. 166 to expose Kaelo's **hypocrisy**? How does this show Kaelo's **pretense** in that he pretends that there was only one way for him to solve the predicament facing him? How does this emphasize his **insensitivity** towards his daughter and thus make his **rationalization** sound **hollow**?

Applying meanings

1. In what manner does the Oloisudori entourage arrive at Kaelo's home? How does Kaelo behave in front of his son-in-law to be? What **gifts** are given to **each person** in the Kaelo family? How does this **heighten** the **conflict** in the narrative on both sides of the divide?
2. What **motive** does Oloisudori have in the way he dresses, arrives and the gifts he gives? What does this mean about his **values**? How do the girls react to the gifts especially Taiyo? What then are their values? How does Ole Kulet use this to **contrast** the old and the young?
3. What does the reaction of characters to material objects elucidate the theme of **Greed and Materialism**? How does this show how this theme controls characters' **behavior** and **social values** at large?
4. What role does **irony** play in this chapter? How does the author use it to contrast the aspirations of Kaelo and Resian

in their thoughts, hopes and desires? How does this show Kaelo's guilt and sense of **betrayal** on the one hand and Resian **optimism** and sense of focus on the other?

Chapter 14 – Resian's attempted Abduction and Flight.

Oloisudori invites Kaelo and his wife to his *sixth* home to lure them into urging Resian to marry him. He recalls Resian's beauty and how to impress her comparing himself to **Lord Egerton** who, his love unrequited, banished all women from his castle. Conversely, Kaelo recalls over his visit to Oloisudori's home in a flashback. Oloisudori takes the couple to the lavish home being built for Resian. Impressed by the home, Ole Kaelo resolves to force his daughter to marry Oloisudori. The couple teams up with Oloisudori to hatch up a plan for Resian's abduction. They is taken home in one of Oloisudori's magnificent vehicles. Throughout that day and night, Ole Kaelo is eaten up by guilt over what he does to his daughter. He dreams that his daughter has accepted the marriage proposal.

The girls on the other hand hatch a plan to return their gifts. They pack them in a decorated carton. The parents inform Resian of the impending visit and they're surprised she doesn't resist. On the material day, Resian is cheerful and well dressed and ready and everyone agrees that she looks stunning. Oloisudori plans meticulously and arrives on time. He stops at Nasila to review the plan of Resian's abduction with his entourage. Though afraid, Resian plucks up courage and is ready for Oloisudori at the door when he arrives. He is as showy as ever but his appearance ironically disdains the young girl. She receives him and he praises her for 'having taken the decision' to marry him. He goes ahead to tell her about it and when she protests, he informs her that there is nothing she can do.

Resian runs to her father's shop to find out about enrolling at the university which her father refuses flat out. She screams protests at him accusing him of selling her off; he slaps her twice. She is defiant and tells him she'd rather die than marry Oloisudori. She runs away to Nasila River where she contemplates suicide. Olarinkoi comes and promises to take her to Emakererei. He promises to take her to sleep with a certain family, organize transport and take her to Emakererei the next day.

Chapter 15 – Attempted Rape, Circumcision on Resian.

Resian wakes up in an old woman's house, takes breakfast, then the journey begins. She is happy to have outfoxed Oloisudori and her father. The journey is tough with heat and insects giving her hell. She is occupied by thoughts and hope of her reception by Emakererei. Finally, they arrive at a house where the vehicle deposits them before speeding away. Olarinkoi orders her to make food after lighting a lamp. He then leaves her locking the gate from outside. She is worried and wonders what Olarinkoi intends but finally reasons he means well; that he has gone to sleep elsewhere so they can continue their journey in the morning. She drifts off to sleep only to be rudely awakened by the return of a drunk Olarinkoi who drags her to bed, tearing her garments claiming she is his wife from then on, and tries to rape her. He hits her and she falls unconscious.

She comes to to see herself naked in bed and remembers what had happened slowly. She drifts in and out of consciousness and when she becomes fully conscious, she sees an old woman and realizes that the old woman has been taking care of her for some time. It takes several days for her to heal and get out of the house. Towards evening, an ugly woman drives sheep into the homestead. She turns out to be Olarinkoi's mother. She is contemptuous of her and her *intoiye nemengalana* state. She is scornful of both her father and Oloisudori who she says doesn't deserve Resian; it is her son who does and they intend to circumcise her to make her a wife worthy of him. She tells her that she has engaged a circumciser and she and Olarinkoi will move to Tanzania to escape her pursuers. Resian decides to keep strong. She reflects on how things might be going at home pitying her sister and blaming her mother for her silence and abetting her own daughter's exploitation. The moon finds her sitting outside and the *enkabaani* comes. She proceeds to explain about Olarinkoi's mother and her predictions. She says that she and a circumciser had already been paid but she has a change of heart and promises to help Resian.

Chapter 16 – The Escape, Meeting Emakererei.

Olarinkoi's mother accuses Resian of refusing to eat and probes her stomach to ensure she isn't pregnant. She rails against the rich and especially Oloisudori who she helped poach elephant tusks and rhino horns but later abandoned her. Nabaru becomes a close friend and confidant to Resian. Resian is cautious for Nabaru supports of FGM. She ventures outside the homestead, meeting three young women married in the area; they look neglected and are married to men thrice their age.

One day Olarinkoi visits Resian. He regrets having hit her. He informs her that plans are on course to circumcise her in three days. She realizes she has nowhere to run and can't outwit Olarinkoi and his mother; her hope now lies in Nabaru who doesn't come that day and she begins doubting her promise to help her. She sinks into despondency, then drifts into a dream in which she fights circumcisers; the Nasila circumciser, Olarinkoi's mother and Nabaru. She wakes up feverish to a sudden banging on the door. She is just able to open it before falling down unconscious. Nabaru prepares medicine for her and she regains consciousness. She understands the urgency of flight and the two women go out of the gate in time to see Olarinkoi, his mother and a circumciser approaching. They hurry through the rain to a lorry that Nabaru has procured to take them away. Olarinkoi comes in hot pursuit but they are able to lock themselves inside the cabin of the lorry. The two rail at the angry Olarinkoi.

The lorry sets off on a hazardous journey. It travels through rain on cattle tracks before the weather lets up a little but they later come to the sheep farm of the Emakererei. Nabaru tells Resian how she walked a whole day to the town where she could get the lorry to save her. Resian hugs her gratefully. Three motorcycle riders arrive and one of them turns out to be Minik. She is stunning and impresses Resian. She learns from her that Oloisudori and her father advertised her desertion and put a bounty of half-a-million shillings on her. She orders the driver to bring Resian to her offices. Resian is briefly put off by the said advertisement but it serves to strengthen her resolve; no one will sway her charted course.

She recalls the words of 1 Corinthians 13:12 which strengthen her determination.

Commentary

Oloisudori uses his vast wealth to bully and lure people in order to get his way. He impresses Kaelo and his wife so as to get them to coax Resian to marry him. The reminiscences of both Oloisudori and Kaelo show their worship of material things. The author mocks at Ole Kaelo's justification of his God-given duty to ensure his daughter marries well – even without her consent. The author is sarcastic of Oloisudori's time-consciousness; it is inspired by his criminal activities. He assumes that Resian's amiable behavior is an acceptance of his marriage proposal. The clash between father and daughter comes to its zenith. Resian's contemplation of suicide shows the extremes to which she has been forced by society. Olarinkoi comes to intensify the conflict with a false promise of saving her.

Resian's **internal conflict** intensifies when Olarinkoi takes her to a deserted house and leaves without explanation. Nabaru, who takes care of her after the attempted rape, stresses the need for women to stand together. Amid threats by Olarinkoi's mother, Resian resolves to remain mentally strong and fight. Her strength of mind and body endears her to her nurse and she promises to help her symbolizing *how women should unite to fight a common enemy*. They run away and the journey is quite hazardous symbolizing *the resolve that women need to have to free themselves*. Their journey is crowned with finally meeting Minik ene Nkoitoi. She is not only beautiful but impressive in her strength of mind and authority. Resian's steadfastness are rewarded with her arrival and acceptance at the sheep farm; avoiding FGM and joining college is now a near certainty.

Identifying Important facts.

1. How does Ole Kaelo go about rationalizing the abduction and marrying off of his daughter? Why doesn't he make this decision before now? What then is his **motive** in making this resolve? Describe the final conflict between father and daughter.
2. How does Ole Kulet show the **maturing** character of Resian in this chapter? Use two adjectives to capture the changing characters of Ole Kaelo, Oloisudori and Resian in chapter 14.
3. How is Feminism brought out in this chapter in the following ways;

i. Decisions being made for Resian by other people.
ii. Resian's life being determined by others and her ambitions being curtailed.
iii. Resian's defiance of her father and running away from the arranged marriage?

1. Identify two instances of the use of the following aspects of style;

i. Situational irony
ii. Sarcasm
iii. Foreshadowing
iv. Symbolism and imagery

Interpreting Facts to get Meaning

1. How does Olarinkoi heighten the **conflict** in chapter 15?

What role do Olarinkoi's mother and the *enkabaani* play in *intensifying the conflict*?

2. Resian's fight in question 2 above is **physical**. How does this fight extend in a more forceful way in chapter 15? What **character traits** of Resian does the author emphasize this way? What point does the author therefore make about **a woman's body and mind**?
3. How is **feminism** stressed in Resian's **taking her life in her own hands**? What point about feminism does the author make through Olarinkoi's mother and the enkabaani?
4. How relevant is the use of biblical allusion in chapter 15? How else is imagery and symbolism used elsewhere in the chapter and with what effect?

Applying Meanings

1. What do you think is the role of the hazardous journey and the rain as Resian and the *enkabaan*i escape from Olarinkoi? Enumerate the other problems that Resian is faced with.
2. How do the problems facing Resian help in growth/maturity of her character? What do you think is Kulet's point? How is Resian a symbol of other girls facing similar situations? Use five **adjectives** qualifying character traits required in any young girl facing Resian's situation.
3. What themes emerge in chapter 16? How are they united in the larger question of **the girl child**? What **morals** do we learn through them?
4. Identify use of **biblical allusion** in chapter 16. Read through *these verses* and say how they **capture** Resian's state. What does Ole Kulet's invocation of religion mean here in terms of character and theme?

Chapter 17 – Minik's welcome, Nabaru's change.

Resian and Nabaru are driven to Minik. She meets Minik and boldly states her case. Minik welcomes her to and she takes a bath. She relates her troubles and Taiyo's to Minik's listening ear. Minik tells Nabaru she wouldn't criticize her for believing in FGM. She elucidates the negative elements of the rite giving examples of other rites that had been discarded because they had outlived their usefulness. Eventually, Nabaru agrees with her and vows to join her in campaigning for the end of FGM. Minik thanks Resian for her modesty and bravery and promises to ensure she joins the university she has longed for. She is also rewarded with a job, a house, a scholarship and an advance salary to enable her buy dresses. She is then taken to the comfortable house which Minik gives her and she emotionally hugs and thanks her. Mink inducts her into her work over the days that follow. Resian devotes herself to her new work which she gives undivided attention which pleases her mentor immensely.

Chapter 18 – Taiyo's Rescue, Parmuat's Death

Resian has been working at the farm for five days. A vehicle arrives at the farm bringing a victim of FGM. Minik explains how they rescued her but the man who had helped them was killed. It turns out that the rescued girl is Resian only sister, Taiyo, and the dead man is none other than Joseph Parmuat. Taiyo reflects on how she was induced into FGM through the tacit agreement of her mother. Three women lie to her that her sister has been located but she won't eat; they therefore want to take her to persuade Resian to eat. She only realizes that she has been tricked when it is too late.

The girls finally meet and there is an emotional reunion. Taiyo heals slowly and in two weeks, she is able to get out of bed. In their reflections, the girls blame their father for their misery. They also blame their mother for her docility. Taiyo heals enough to accept her condition and engage in heated debate with the others over FGM.

They all agree that women are their own enemy. Nabaru urges Taiyo to accept her condition but ensure it happens to no one else.

Chapter 19 – Admission to Egerton, Rebuffing Oloisudori.

Minik summons the girls to her office and informs them that they have been admitted to Egerton University. She holds a celebration to bid them farewell. The eating and drinking is crowned by the song which underscores the girls' achievements. They are proud, educated professionals ready to build their nation alongside their male counterparts. The party is ruined by the arrival of Oloisudori and his entourage. He bluntly states that he has come for either of the girls for he has already paid dowry. Minik defies him and when his men try to grab Resian, Oloisudori and his men are beaten up and their vehicles burnt down; they have to run for their lives. The following day, the two girls leave the sheep farm for Egerton University amid celebration by one and all.

Commentary

Resian arrival at the Ntare-Naaju, the hot bath and changing clothes symbolizes a new start. Her strength is seen in that despite the horrendous experiences, she comes out with a strong mind. Minik recognizes her strength and bravery and the age difference between her, Resian and Nabaru, which would allow Nabaru to hold different values. Resian is also gladly rewarded symbolizing what is in store for gallant soldiers like her. Her commitment to her new work speaks volumes of her character and greatly foreshadows her future commitment to her work, her education and to other people.

Through Taiyo's experience, we see how family is often culpable in the abuse of girls. Her traumatic experience is made possible by her mother. Resian, Minik and Nabaru together help Taiyo heal. They underscore the need for all women to support each other. It is clear that women are their own enemies and that those who have undergone FGM should accept themselves the way they are but they must fight to bring the tradition to an end.

The girls' endurance is finally crowned by admission to the university. The party shows that their success is a win for everyone. The invitation of the primary school children serves to inspire them and show the need for education. Their song summarize the themes of the novel. The girl child is liberated, educated and ready to build the nation. The clash between Oloisudori and Minik is the epitome of women liberation. The burning of vehicles symbolizes destruction of macho structures that yoke women. Indeed, Oloisudori and his cohorts' flight signifies utter defeat of such structures while the departure of the two girls the following day is the symbolic crowning of the girls child – a pointer to the role of education in women empowerment.

Identifying Important Facts

1. Why is it vital for Resian to **relate** what she experiences? Why would you want to **know** such details if you were in Minik's shoes? What point does Ole Kulet make in Nabaru's changing her point of view?
2. Briefly relate how Minik **receives** Resian and Nabaru. Point out details that show she is **patient** but **authoritative**.
3. Why are **male characters** deliberately left out of the picture in this chapter? Why does the story specifically focus on the three women?
4. Why do you think 95 percent of the story in this chapter comes via **narration**? How does this affect the reception of the narrative?

Interpreting Facts to get Meaning.

1. Who is to blame for what happens to Taiyo? What do you think is the author's **point** in presenting two sisters, one circumcised and the other not and having them accept their **condition** in the end?
2. What other **character** of Minik do we see through the way she receives Taiyo? How does she go about breaking the news of Taiyo's condition to her sister? How does this balance her **authoritative** side?
3. Male characters fade away in the last character to leave positive women characters. How does the author tone down this positive aspect of women in chapter 18? How does this help create **verisimilitude** in the narrative? What role do you think Joseph Parmuat plays in this chapter?
4. What **role** does **flashback** play in integrating the narrative here? How does it help emphasize the trauma that Taiyo goes through?

Applying Meanings

1. What would you say are the two **major events** in chapter 19? Which major characters feature in each event? In what ways is the last chapter a '**clash of the titans**'?
2. Use **opposite adjectives** to capture the character of Minik and Oloisudori considering;

i. Wealth versus humility
ii. Threats versus action
iii. Patient wisdom versus rash anger

1. Though the last chapter makes a big point about **women empowerment**, how does the author show that male participation is imperative in this endeavor? How does education lead to such empowerment and how do outdated

traditions curtail it?

2. **Contrast and juxtaposition** plays a big role in this chapter. How does the author draw contrast through;

i. Events
ii. Characters and their age
iii. Winning and losing?

CHARACTERS AND CHARACTERISATION

A character is an actor in a work of literature. In fiction, characters are generally people like us; they eat and drink, love and hate, live and die. (See note on characterization). There are two ways of creating a character. In **direct** or **explicit** characterization, the writer tells you directly what a character is like. This can be done through the narrator, another character or even by the character him/herself. In **indirect** or **implicit** characterization, you will need to infer or make educated guesses for yourself to see what a character is like by carefully examining a character's speech, action or behavior, thoughts, appearance as well as how s/he relates with others. You should also examine what other characters say about a particular character and how they treat him/her. This must be done wisely for some characters may be naïve, wicked or wrong. Character traits will be revealed to us in six main ways;

1. We may be told openly what a character is; *(Ole Kaelo) had a contentious mind that seemed to question every aspect of his life.*
2. Characters may be made to behave in a certain way so that we make conclusions about them. When we are told *He was gesticulating violently apparently reprimanding orders* we learn that Ole Kaelo is **irascible** and **intimidating**.
3. Often, we learn of a character from what s/he says. When Ole Kaelo says: *Everything is moving on smoothly...* we learn that he is **confident.**

4. A writer may describe how a character *looks* and *dresses* or *keeps his things* that tells us something about them. When we read *The golden chain that dangled from his neck, the golden bracelet and the golden wrist watch, all glittered brilliantly in the morning sunshine'* we learn Oloisudori is **flashy**, **showy** and **ostentatious**.
5. Another way a character trait can be revealed is by the author letting us into his/her mind so that we spy on their thoughts and feelings and thus learn something about them. For example, '*What he thought was going to be a battle of nerves, had turned out to be a walk over. But that did not unduly surprise him. In fact he had nearly expected it...*' we learn that Oloisudori is **full of himself**, **proud** and **overconfident**.
6. Lastly, we learn of a character from what other characters **say** or **think** about the character in question, sometimes from the way they **treat** them. For example, Oloisudori's **greed** and **materialism** is suggested by the thoughts of Ole Kaelo's daughters...It was therefore an insult to their intelligence, dignity and integrity to think that mere material things such as the gifts he lavishly gave them would sway them...'

Apart from the first instance, we have to infer the nature of a character in all other instances. Sometimes, we may require collaborative evidence from elsewhere or a second or even third opinion. For example, as observed above, a third party may tell a lie, they may be mean or they may simply be erroneous. Therefore all such evidence has to be wisely studied before we make decisions.

Characterization is the total process by which a writer creates characters. It includes the entirety of the above factors. When characters don't change between the time we meet them and the time we leave them, we call them **static** characters. Conversely, **dynamic** characters grow with the narrative. **Static** characters who seem the way we've heard other people say or the way we expect such characters to be are referred to as **stereotypes.** Their work is to kowtow to social opinions and they rarely come out alive as personalities. Good writers avoid stereotypes for they add little to the current story; they shine little to us about human nature. A **protagonist** is the leading positive character in a novel, sometimes called the **hero** or **heroine**. The leading **opposite** character is the **antagonist**, sometimes called an **antihero**. A character whose role appears to be to emphasize the qualities of another by contrasting them is called a **foil**. A character **trait** must be seen to be regular before we can use it as a label for a character - we need to also use several occurrences of the display of a trait (or else use collaborative evidence of other traits) before we can confidently use the trait as a label. Character is expressed in **adjectives** – descriptive words which capture the nature of a character so that we can see them in our mind's eye; vain, defiant, well-behaved, even-tempered, lithe, inane, acerbic etc. We must be careful how we use adjectives. Do not say *complaisant* when you mean *complacent* or *discrete* when you mean *discreet*. In the same way, aim at capturing a trait so that your reader 'sees' it. If you think a word will sound pompous and you can't think of a substitute, use a phrase or a list of adjectives that attempts to achieve the same effect. Do not say *cantankerous*; say 'bad-tempered, argumentative, and uncooperative' instead. On the other hand, do not be too simplistic. Do not settle for simple 'good' or 'bad' for these adjectives are not meaningful at all.

A character's **role** is the supposed work/function s/he fulfils within a literary work such as a novel. A character may help emphasize other characters or reveal themes. Examine characters carefully to decide what their use in a piece of writing appears to be. Remember too that fully developed characters play diverse roles. Lastly, you must labor to present an *entire* picture of a character. This includes who they are in terms of social relationships with other characters as well as whom they make themselves as a product of their behavior. Do not portray stereotypes. A good character picture must also look at the pros and cons and comment on whether the particular character is credible or not, whether they are **flat**, **static** or even **stereotypical**. Two things to bear in mind; some adjectives must be cautiously thought about for many adjectives are either past their sell-by dates like last week's bread, or may be confused with their opposite. As observed earlier do not say *sober* when you mean *somber*, *childish* when you mean *childlike*, *chick* when you mean *chic*. Also, use the **present simple tense** to describe character; Resian *is*, rather than Resian *was*, Taiyo *scorns*, instead of Taiyo s*corned*.

Let us now seriously examine some of the leading characters in the novel.

RESIAN

She is arguably the **protagonist** of the novel. We meet her first as she and her sister watch their father as he directs the loading of their belongings as they prepare to leave for Nasila. She is in her late teens, just blossoming into a woman and of the age to go to college; we are given to understand that she is just through with high school and has done well enough to join college. She is Ole Kaelo's second-born daughter and a sister to Taiyo, the first born.

Resian is quite **dynamic**. When we meet her, she is a **naïve** child who is easily cowed by her father and depends on her sister for protection and to voice her opinions especially to her father. She keeps urging her sister to request their father to let them enroll at the Egerton University and is content to wait for feedback. She is an **avid** reader whose face is almost always buried in a book, a fact which her father mistakes for laziness. In the beginning, she is **fragile** and has to lean on her sister for emotional support. She is easily intimidated by her father and trembles when he scolds her. Her mother similarly treats her like a breakable object intervening to make her husband's threats to her daughter a little mild. This underscores her **innocence** bringing out the insensitivity of her father and Oloisudori as they plan her forced marriage. She detects her father's resentment from a young age which makes her **sensitive** and **intuitive**. Her father's attitude also turns her **morose**, confused and offended.

'Resian instinctively detected the absence of love from her father...As a result, her nature was darkened by melancholy. Self-doubt made her awkward and very difficult to deal with.' (pg. 10)

As the narrative continues, Resian pulls her neck out her collar. She becomes more **assertive** and **bold**. When they visit their uncle's home, she is **critical** of some of the things she sees while her sister is content to ignore them in the name of modesty. She notes the competition in the family and the high rate of pregnancy despite the fact that their aunts pretend that everything is alright. She is **inquisitive**, **curious** and **judgmental** openly giving her own opinion about issues. At the uncle's place for example, she gives her honest opinion that exposes the hypocrisy in the home. She keeps and open mind and openly questions the beliefs of her mother and her aunt. She questions the patriarchal status quo insisting that the men in their society need to share responsibilities. She is intelligent and relates the story of the Olarinkoi to the problems of the women in their society while her sister and her mother prefer to hide their heads in the sand.

She remains **determined**, **optimistic**, **committed** and **focused** on her goals. She says from the very beginning that she wants to go to Egerton University to study veterinary medicine. She keeps her mind active through reading and insists that other matters such as marriage and children can wait until she obtains a degree. When she is abducted, she keeps Nabaru talking in order to get as much information as possible so that she can plan her moves. She is optimistic about her escape though her circumstances remain grim, just like she is optimistic that she will one day be a doctor. When she feels that her integrity is being downplayed, she commits herself to resist. She decides to resist circumcision mentally if it gets to a point where the physical act has to be done. When she learns that Oloisudori had placed an advertisement in the papers, she reminds herself to keep focused. 'But as she climbed onto the lorry, she reminded herself of her resolution: she would not allow other people to sway her from her charted course' (256) 'Woe unto him if he thought....daughter of Ole Kaelo to reckon with' (196)

She is **argumentative**, **opinionated** and **resolute**. She says that men should cook and is not afraid to voice her opinion in front of her mother and her aunt though she can clearly see that they are intimidated and prefer to live the way their patriarchal society dictates. Her mother considers her obstinate and defiant and admits that Resian has an **independent** mind. When her father tries to silence her helping to cook, she argues with him and he is forced to silence her by getting physical. She argues with her mother about letting visitors dictate to them about how they should be treated until her parents have to see her way. The same is seen when she visits her father at the shop and stands her ground about going to the university. This time round, her father has to silence her by slapping her. She tells her father that she'd rather die than marry a bank robber; she declares that she'll have to go to the university even if it will happen when she's eighty.

She is **loving** to her family and especially to her sister. She agonizes about what Taiyo goes through when she disappears. Later, she breaks down when her sister is brought to the sheep farm.

Resian plays the **role** of emphasizing the way the youth especially girls need to go. Though she fails to get love at home, she keeps her chin up and determines her life letting no one tell her otherwise. Through her, the author shows how strong young girls need to be in order to change the society. She stands up to the hype of both her society and her parents and refuses to let her life be determined by them. She keeps her head focused on her goals despite having all manner of odds against her. It takes a lot of courage to say no to her father, run away from home and fight both Olarinkoi and Oloisudori. It is a great wonder that she comes out of it all unscathed.

TAIYO

An older sister to Resian and of age to go to college too, Taiyo finds herself the protector of her younger sister and therefore balances between her sister's obstinate nature and the **model naïve, obedient** child that their parents want them to be. She is her sister's protector and shields her emotionally from a loveless father and a lukewarm mother. She is docile and **submissive** to her parents playing an understanding companion to her intimidated mother from whom she learns to be submissive and to respect her father in spite of his excesses. She however finds herself at odds with her society and her family when she falls in love with Joseph Parmuat, a thing that is prohibited by her society, but one which she is unable to extricate herself from.

When we meet her, she is **tactful**, **docile**, **obedient** and **respectful** to her parents. She is her father's **popular** child and is **careful** not to be antagonistic with either of her parents. She therefore bids her time when she wants to talk to her father, for example, waiting until she thinks he is approachable. She also takes it as her duty to ask favors on behalf of her sister because she knows her father's open attitude to her and therefore reduces the antagonism at home. She considers her sisters bold, argumentative nature as an immature disrespect for her parents and her society and chides her severally about it.

She is **industrious**, **hardworking** and **determined** at school. Like her sister, she works hard and passes her exams and we are given to believe that she is only waiting for her father's nod to join the university. She is also adept at music and dance which she does well enough to be recognized by an FM radio station and get a chance to attend a music extravaganza at the coast. When her father agrees to their being taught music by Joseph Parmuat, she takes to it like a fish to water and spends quite a lot of time trying to learn from him.

She is **bold**, **courageous** and **protective**. She stands up to her father when she asks for permission to attend the music extravaganza, arguing with him though she doesn't get the permission. 'She had stubbornly put up a spirited struggle but the battle was so predictably and utterly lost.' She boldly comes between father and daughter to get their father to see their point of view. When attacked by a strange man, she trembles in anger and demands to be let go.

She is an **inquisitive happy-go-lucky** child who is sometimes **cunning**, **humorous** and **mischievous**. She easily falls in love with Joseph Parmuat and does not shy away from expressing her feelings despite the fact that her type of society is likely to raise eyebrows. When he shies away, she boldly confronts him at his house and makes him see that they do not have to conform to what she regards as backward demands of her society; Parmuat has to agree with her. She digs information about the Olarinkoi from the reluctant Parmuat, mischievously creating humorous innuendos which set him at ease. She dances with reckless abandon, holding her head haughtily and gyrating her hips to goad and challenge him.

She is **open** about her feelings and **practical** about conduct becoming **scornful** and **sardonic** about some beliefs of her society. She is scornful about the reality of the *patureishi* and sardonic about basics of Nasila culture she deems archaic. She thinks Nasila culture abhorrent because it doesn't respect her rights. She is **defiant** of it and thinks it denies her rights for no reason at all. She is similarly open to her sister who she openly regards as infantile when she doesn't exhibit maturity. She criticizes her for running to the garden and openly competing with adults without respecting either their feelings or opinions. She is however **loving** and **supportive** to her. She shares her feelings about Oloisudori and **conspiratorially** plans to return his gifts. Resian herself pities her sister's ever ready attitude to listen to her troubles and sooth her anger.

In spite of her boldness, she remains sensitive and human. She is embarrassed when Parmuat finds her snooping at his rooms. It is her childlike curiosity that drives her to look at how he lives. She also stands by her sister and is willing to venture into the unknown to rescue her.

Taiyo plays a **supportive role** to Resian in her quest for self-determination. She balances the characters of her parents and that of her sister and shows that girl children can rise up and continue with life even after they have fallen. Despite being circumcised, she is able to accept her condition and continue with her education vowing to prevent what has happened to her happening to others especially her children.

PARSIMEI OLE KAELO

A retrenched husband and father of two college bound girls, Ole Kaelo finds himself at two crossroads; first, he is at an age crossroad where he represents a dying age while having to deal with daughters focused on a future. Second, he is at a cultural crossroad where he has to remain true to a dying tradition but house daughters of the new age. His economic troubles come to define his destiny though this is refined by his **high-handed** rule of his household.

Like all naïve retirees, he is trapped by a cunning Oloisudori into setting up a business using borrowed funds and ideas. In his **shortsightedness**, he doesn't study these ideas and as a result, he pays heavily for his naivety. We are given to believe he is **trustworthy** and

scrupulous through his dealings with Ole Supeyo and this is one way in which his naivety is exposed. He is **too trusting** both of his culture, his society and his friends whose activities or opinions he doesn't question. He comes out as **sensitive** and **culture-conscious** to the extent of preferring to be in conflict with his family in order to maintain an acceptable social mien. He shifts his family from Nakuru to Nasila in order to 'return to his people' as it were. He not only builds a home among his people but he also holds a homecoming ceremony in which he is welcomed back by the elders in the right manner. In his culture-consciousness, he comes to hate his daughter who he sees as the son that never was and comes into conflict with his two daughters as he insists on their undergoing circumcision and marrying the traditional way. We are given to understand however that part of this is driven by what he owes Oloisudori.

He begins as trustworthy and **honest**, **meticulous** and **aggressively industrious**. He works hard to provide for his family and helps his friend Ole Supeyo in his business activities. He has a shrewd brain and works hard to rise through the ranks to become a manager. Ole Supeyo comes to trust him because though the latter is illiterate, Ole Kaelo does not misdeal him. This trust however works against him. He is quick to trust others and is therefore easily taken advantage of by knaves such as Oloisudori. He also drives people to the wall in his meticulous demand for perfection. He drives his workers like donkeys and a similar attitude leads his children to fear him so that they run to the kitchen when he comes home and are unable to approach him when they want his help. They are afraid of reporting the attack on them because they fear he will criticize them for '...having dared to venture into an unknown territory without his approval.' (20)

He is **abusive** and **impatient**. He has no patience with his workers and fusses about, curses and mutters under his breath when they cannot seem to work quickly enough. He has no patience with Resian who he thinks is slow to think and to behave despite her showing signs of adulthood. He is **greedy** for quick riches which drives him to trust Oloisudori and be tricked by him. In the same way, he is **materialistic** and is taken in by Oloisudori's wealth, his shiny vehicles as well as the pretended friendship. He is after quick profit and establishes a big shop while building a palatial home with no clear ways to pay for them.

He has a **cunning** way of rationalizing issues and a **hypocritical** and **pretentious** way of seeing only one solution to his problems. He rationalizes his following Oloisudori though he knows the latter's unpalatable business activities. 'Whoever wanted to eat meat, must of necessity dance to the music of the man who held the knife' (25). In a similar manner, he rationalizes his hate for his daughter so that it becomes easier on his conscience to marry her off. 'Signs of early womanhood were evident. The earlier he disposed of her, he declared to himself angrily, the better'. (10). Like Oloisudori, he is **boastful** and **ostentatious**. He boasts about his contracts though they have not yet been realized. He puts up a showy business and builds a palatial home on borrowed funds with no sure guarantee of returns. He is pompous both in speech and in manner. (69). He brings Olarinkoi to his house but does not bother to inform his family what his terms of engagement are. He gets both Olarinkoi and Joseph Parmuat to teach his daughters about their culture without the tacit knowledge of his daughters or his wife. He tells his daughter that her future is important to him when he openly disregards her opinions. He pretends to give Resian a number of options available at the university ostensibly to show there is no hurry in enrolling while he knows very well he wants her married.

He worships Oloisudori and his wealth. He is thoroughly intimidated in the latter's presence and behaves like a nervous dog before its master. He clasps his hands as if in prayer and shuffles his feet in Oloisudori's presence. He licks his lips and wets his eyes when he sees Oloisudori's glittering vehicle. He is **timid** and throws glances at his daughters as if to warn them not to embarrass him in Oloisudori's presence.

Ole Kaelo plays the **role** of an **insensitive parent** showing how parents betray their children for material gain. Despite his education, he resorts to culture and tradition so as to hypocritically get a leeway to marry off his daughter and thereby gain the riches he covets. Ole Kulet uses him as a symbol of the length to which greed and materialism can drive an individual.

EDWARD OLOISUDORI LOONKIYAA

A picture of **pompous**, **shallow** intelligence, Oloisudori Loonkiyaa is as **showy** as his name sounds. He is full of himself and believes everyone must genuflect to him for he is rich and can buy anything he desires. He is a corrupt criminal who has used the *enkaiboni's* home as a conduit for poached ivory and rhino horns. We learn too that he has been in and out of jail and is an incurable extortionist. He is **materialistic** and uses gifts to entice people into his traps. He comes carrying impressive gifts to the Kaelo home so as to get Kaelo and his wife to work his way. He then takes them on a tour of his new home to entice them into convincing their daughter to marry him.

He is **polygamous** and has no respect for any of his wives. He believes marrying a woman is a battle which he has to win by whatever means necessary. He looks down on all women who he sees as chattels meant to entertain him at his will. His six wives are put through a test which suggests he plays them like toys. 'For him to accept any of them, each had to fulfil certain conditions and agree to live a certain pattern of life.' (202) Ole Supeyo describes him as corrupt and only does business when it suits him. He warns Kaelo of Oloisudori's **immoral** nature comparing him to a randy he-goat.

He is **extravagant** and **ostentatious**. He arrives at the Kaelo home in gleaming vehicles clad in golden objects meant to entice the family. He is **brusque** and **intimidating**. He does not wait to be invited but brushes against the young girl's bosom into the house. He is **immodest** and **immoral**. He ogles Resian openly not hiding his open lust for her in spite of her being young enough to be his daughter. At the sheep farm, he arrives in a convoy of about ten vehicles and an entourage of men. He is **self-assured** and believes that his wealth can buy him anything he desires. When Resian mocks him, he is sarcastic of her and openly laughs at her and calls her his wife with an unquestioned finality. 'Whether you scream your heart out, or jump into the deep sea, Resian, you are mine. You are my wife from now henceforth' (204). He is a bully who believes he can get his way around despite what other people feel or think.

Oloisudori plays the **role** of the **insensitive polygamist** who has no qualms about how he treats any of the women he marries. He is a rough child abuser who insists on his own way because apparently, he thinks money and wealth can take him wherever he desires to go.

JOSEPH PARMUAT

A young teacher at a primary school in Nasila and a trainer in music and dance, he has a rich cultural heritage which he imparts on fellow age mates and children. His house shows that he is **neat**, tidy, **orderly** and **well read** – the reason for his wide knowledge on culture. He is **impressive** in manner, speech and dance which captures Taiyo's eye and endears the young man to her. He is described as **tall, young** and **handsome**. He believes in the culture of his people which he trusts to guide him in life. He is happy to take part in cultural dances and to teach the same to children at the school where he works.

He is a **free** and **easy-going** spirit. He is **committed** to the girls when he begins teaching them traditional song and dance. He is especially free with Taiyo with whom he becomes **friendly** and finally falls in love. He is however **dignified, cautious** but **caring**. He takes care not to do anything that might annoy Ole Kaelo who he regards as a father. He also takes care not to get too intimate with Taiyo who he can easily see is head over heels for him. He understands his culture and knows what the punishment for indecency would be.

He is **cunning** and **clever**. Seeing Taiyo try to put a bug in his ear, he learns to avoid being alone with her knowing well what it could lead to. He is **committed** to duty and to his friends. He takes the job of teaching the girls seriously while observing the limits of what his job entails. He is **knowledgeable** of his culture and **humorous** in looking for ways to explain some of the things the girls wouldn't fathom. He for example, has a humorous way of explaining the origin of Olarinkoi – the real and fantastic which leaves Taiyo is stitches. He is **caring** of his people and their culture. He is **concerned** that their culture is changing especially thinking of the rise of egoism and petty jealousy. He is **practical** about the culture but criticizes it for forbidding the kind of love he has for Taiyo. He argues that it isn't static for it has shed many negative aspects. He also tells the girls to accept the fact that very soon they'll see people coming to their home to try and marry them. He is reluctant to discuss love because he knows there is little he and Taiyo can do about the already set standards. He is **sincere** about his own feelings and **passionate** when he hugs Taiyo but finally decides that culture knows best and he must submit himself to it.

Joseph Parmuat plays the **role** of a **young guide** to the Kaelo girls. He shows it is possible to remain chaste and modest, respectful and respected in the way he handles his duty given him by Ole Kaelo. He is inspiring in the way he dies trying to save Taiyo and contrasts the insensitivity of the older generation of Kaelo, Oloisudori and Olarinkoi; he is sacrificing.

MINIK ENE NKOITOI

The Emakererei, Minik is an **admirable** woman who not only inspires the youth to stand up for what they believe in but also impresses the reader in the way she rebuffs the likes of the feared Oloisudori. Her reputation precedes her and we hear of her long before we set eyes on her. She is well **educated**, having gone as far as Makerere in Uganda which gave her the name and having been employed as the manager of the sheep farm Ntare-Naaju. She is brave in not only being the only voice that condemns FGM but also in the fact that she is the only one who has the guts to put up a physical place to which the emotionally wounded girls like Resian can run. The arrival of Oloisudori and his entourage speaks a lot about the courage required to do so.

She comes out as **far sighted** and **pioneering**. She sees the use of education in women empowerment early enough and takes advantage of the same. It is this which leads her to become a leading light which many girls look up to. She sets the pace and the likes of Resian and Taiyo follow eagerly in her footsteps.

She is described as **strong**, **firm** and beautiful. She comes riding on a motorcycle yet this does not diminish her **femininity**. Her strength is emphasized by her build and her posture. She is slightly built but her shoulders and back are straight and she carries and 'aura of superiority and authority around her' (255). She is **humorous** in the way she makes fun of serious issues to keep Resian at peace, '...don't you lose her for she is worth a lot of money!' (256). Her mental strength is further emphasized by her gait and the way she carries her chin. He big eyes give her look the air of a 'physical force'.

In spite of this, she is **humble**, **welcoming** and **sensitive** to the needs of the girls. She is **hospitable** to Resian who she gives a comfortable house and a job symbolizing the need to take care of both physical and emotional needs of women. She is **caring** in the way she receives Taiyo and the way she goes about breaking the news of her arrival and the death of Parmuat to Resian. In spite of this, her strength is well seen in the way she faces up to Oloisudori and the way she commands the farm not to mention her handling the issues of rescuing girls and sending Resian and Taiyo to the university.

Minik largely plays the **role** of **inspiration** both to the fictional characters in the novel and to real girls who might require her kind of inspiration. She shows that where there is a will, there is a way in the way she single-handedly stands up to FGM and authoritatively deals with the likes of Oloisudori.

OLARINKOI

A mobile **mystery**, he is symbolic of the many issues which stand in the way of women's liberation but which society can still not put a finger on. The way he emerges from nowhere and becomes a thorn in Resian's flesh suggests the lack of will to examine what really ails women in the society – mostly by the men - sometimes by the women themselves. His arrival at the Kaelo home is as mysterious as his departure and at one point we are given to think that he is playing the same role as Joseph Parmuat.

He is quite **hypocritical** in the way he remains in the background playing his cards until he can strike at the right moment. He is **cunning** in the way he helps the girls to gain their confidence so that Resian doesn't question his offer for help at all. He feigns concern when he finds her at the river and lies about Emakererei to win her confidence. He greets Resian and the old woman cheerfully only to change and become **brutal** when he gets her home. His hypocritical and pretentious nature is emphasized by his getting drunk, something Resian hadn't witnessed before. He becomes **rude** and **abusive** when he has her where he wants. He is **lustful** and **insensitive** in trying to rape her as well as brutal in his attack.

He plays the **role** of the **silent criminal**. He pretends throughout the time he lives with the girls only to turn worse than Oloisudori when he has the chance. His hypocrisy is further emphasized by the fact that we learn from his mother that he may have been planning the abduction longer than Oloisudori himself. He emphasizes the fact that still waters run deep; most of the dangers facing young girls are next to them and are wolves in sheepskin.

JANE MILANOI

She is Ole Kaelo's wife and a mother to Taiyo and Resian. She's been married to Ole Kaelo for twenty-two years. Unemployed, she relies on her husband for the upkeep of the family. When he is retrenched, therefore, she has no choice but to agree with him about the need to relocate and begin a new life.

She is **naïve** for she neither questions her husband preparedness but takes his assurance as gospel truth. She doesn't question how much money he has, how much goes to the shop or how much goes into putting up a new home. It therefore comes as a surprise to her when she learns that her husband's wealth is tagged to Oloisudori and that the latter demands to marry their daughter. She doesn't think about what her daughters will face in the new town and dismisses as 'busy bodies' those who question her about the status of her daughters. She realizes too late that those people could be her future relatives. Though circumcised herself, she can't see the possible effect of the force ritual on her daughters in modern times neither can she comprehend the effect of marrying them off to men they dislike or stopping their education. She is **fatalistic** and **pessimistic**. She doesn't think of any way to deal with Oloisudori though she sees very well that what he does to them is wrong. She blindly supports the old system of things which makes men like Oloisudori exploit her and sees no way out.

She is **vain** and likes to keep up with the Joneses. When she hears of her husband's intention to put up the shop, what comes to mind first is 'a chance to be associated with the great and the powerful of the land'. She also hopes to marry off her two daughters to reputable sons-in-law in the new town. Similarly, she is taken in by Oloisudori's opulence and showy manner especially after he takes them on a trip of his homes.

She is the **perfect housewife**. She keeps out of her husband's business affairs only becoming useful in coking or helping pack luggage. She is **docile** and **submissive**. She doesn't query her husband authority even when he goes against their daughters wishes. She goes along with him when he suggests that they get circumcised and Resian be married to Oloisudori. She is **fragile** and depends on her daughters for protection. When the lorry breaks down on the way to Nasila, it is her daughters who shield her rather than the other way round. This suggests she's delicate and in no position to put up a fight for her daughters when their father becomes authoritative.

She plays the **role** of the **cowardly housewife** who abets the abuse of her children by men within and without the home. She is partly liable for the way Resian turns out because she cannot stand up to her husband. Through her, the author shows how women are largely their own enemies. She is a **foil** to Yeiyo-botorr in the latter's good management of her large family and home.

OLE SUPEYO

We meet him when Ole Kaelo goes to visit him for advice about Oloisudori. He is an old man who is well tempered in business over the years. He is **industrious** and works hard over the years to create personal wealth. He is **patient** and begins with a few cows which he walks to the Dagoreti market before he gets money to start other businesses and invest in farming.

Though old, he is **intelligent** and manages to mix the old and the new. He sends his children to school, even to the university, though he has his daughters circumcised. He is also polygamous with many children. He marries his daughters off early to prominent men in the community and is as incensed about Minik as anyone else. He sends her away when she comes to persuade him to stop circumcising his daughters believing she's a great threat to Maa culture for circumcision is a good rite of passage used to tame a wild gender.

Through him, the author shows that there is a **middle ground** between the old and the new way of life. He shows too that those who curtail the education of their daughters, circumcise them and marry them off are just hypocritical and act out of self-interest. He represents the old school who still blindly believe in the goodness of some aspects of culture which they don't question. He is also used to shine a torch on the naiveté of Ole Kaelo and the hypocrisy and extortionist nature of Oloisudori.

Other minor characters include Nabaru. She is **caring** and **helpful** to Resian during her trying moment. She keeps her from loneness and **conspiratorially** plans her escape. She is **dynamic** in that she finally agrees that FGM is obnoxious and vows to help curb it.

Olarinkoi's mother is a **cruel, old fashioned** hag caricatured as a witch who takes advantage of young girls and enjoys their misery. She is **hypocritical** for she doesn't believe in the goodness of culture; she uses it as a trade and Resian's abduction to her in a mere means of fulfilling a prophesy. Her hypocrisy is also seen in her abetting poaching, only abusing and criticizing Oloisudori because he runs away without paying her.

THEMES

What is a theme? All literary writers write to communicate themes, that is, their thoughts or opinions on certain debatable issues. Themes are controversial ideas about life about which you can have a discussion with somebody because there are no hard rules about how these issues should be handled. Think about modern arguments about devolution and the senate and Governors and County governments in Kenya today. When these ideas were muted, they seemed rosy things that would immediately transform our country into a modern Roman Empire. These ideas have raised controversies because government and leadership are controversial. Anybody can give their opinions for or against them. That is why they are themes.

A theme can be seen as an idea for which, if somebody asked you for your opinion, you would readily say something. A minute later, you will feel tempted to add something else, possibly even to contradict yourself. With a theme, you can never have a decisive debate unless you are one of those stubborn people with whom no one can hold a debate. Leadership as a theme for example has held people in awe since the times of the Egyptian pharaohs, the great Chinese wall and beyond. People are still discussing its nature, going through the motions of refining it (and often doing worse damage), trying to decide which is the best way to lead in order to be fair to all.

A good way to see a theme is to look at its possibilities. If a theme is an opinion, it must be based on *something,* some *idea* that can be captured in one or two words. That idea can be called a **subject**. There are as many subjects as you can care to name; all those things that control how the world goes about its business from day to day - all those ideas for which it is possible to give an opinion. While a subject can be captured in a word or two – science, education, war, marriage, childhood, leadership, etc. (probably even Governorship or *Senatorship* in Kenya!) – a theme can only be captured in a statement. This is because a theme is a person's considered opinion about a subject.

Of science one could say *Science is a mirage that pretends to make life easier while actually making it more difficult*. Of marriage, like Benjamin Disraeli, one could say *Every woman should marry, but no man.* These are opinions.

In literature, themes are writers' opinions about subjects especially the most readily debatable subjects - ones which have been debated over time. Many writers discuss their opinions on subjects which are very close to people's hearts, those with us every day. For many of these subjects, one can have several opinions, especially with wide subjects which touch several aspects of people's lives. All of a writer's opinions on a certain subject can be seen as that writer's theme(s). With wide subjects, it is possible to write several statements which capture what a writer thinks to form a paragraph or a page or even more. This can be seen as a discussion of that theme in a work of literature. What writers do in a novel such as *Blossoms of the Savannah* is to think carefully about their opinions on given subjects, then create a story that validates those opinions in same way we choose a narrative in Oral Literature to teach about say, greed, or treachery. The difference is that in a novel, the writer creates characters who are more or less like us and who encounter situations like the ones we encounter every day. Ours as literature students is to consider the story or stories, identify the characters and their situations and then decipher or interpret – with reasoned arguments – what the writer might be trying to say about his/her opinions on the discussed subjects.

A good, simple way of doing this is to brainstorm with yourself or with others. Pick the characters and list them under the common events which they are involved in. For a subject such as greed, list all those characters who appear to be involved in greed under two titles, the greedy and the righteous, then consider how each character is treated as a result of his greed or righteousness. How do they begin when the play opens? What events do they go through? How do they end up? What does their treatment seem to suggest about the playwright's opinion of the subject of greed and the way it affects people? The statements you come up with can be discussed with ample illustrations to see the playwright's message to you about greed as a subject. This should be the goal of any literature student in discussing themes.

If you list these ideas, events and the characters involved with each theme carefully, you will see that there will be some ideas with more to write about than others. These are the main ideas/themes. The less there is to write about, the less the characters used to illustrate a certain theme, the less significant the treatment by the writer and arguably, the less important it will be.

Considered this way, Henry Ole Kulet's Blossoms *of the Savannah* discusses a many themes. As happens with many authors, Ole Kulet begins with the overriding theme of **women empowerment**, just like John Steinbeck focuses on **greed and materialism** in *The Pearl*. Even so, Ole Kulet finds himself discussing many other themes, especially those which in one way or another are related to the main theme e.g., stopping FGM is central to women empowerment. Think of the theme here in terms of the argument; a different person can present the same argument but under a different title.

Let us now look at some of those themes in detail.

Women Empowerment

This may also be called feminism – a word that refers to the discussion of women issues. *Blossoms of the Savannah* discusses a number of issues that pertain to women in the Maa community. It shows the condition of adult women, the aspirations of the girl child central to which is stopping FGM, and suggests the way forward and gives symbolic suggestions for change.

As the narrative begins, the society is highly patriarchal. This is shown by how Ole Kaelo maintains a firm authority on his family making Mama Milanoi a submissive housewife. She is denied economic power and this in turn denies her a say in how the house hold is run. Ole Kaelo decides where they live and what type of work they engage in. He decides who their neighbors are going to be and therefore effectively controls their opinion. His daughters on the other hand are intimidated by their father who decides how their lives are going to turn out and gives them little leeway to make decisions. They cannot go to college without his nod and that means their lives are suspended between the time the story opens and the time they run away from home. Though they are mature, he makes it his business to have them 'inducted' into the Nasila culture in readiness for their being circumcised and married off. He goes ahead as to choose who marries them when he takes dowry and tries to force Resian to marry Oloisudori. To assert themselves and have a life of their own, the girls are forced to run away from home.

Life among the people of Nasila follows a more or less similar pattern. Ole Supeyo does not educate his daughters and gives them a raw deal because while they get circumcised and married early, his sons are allowed to go to school; two are in fact at the university. The Simiren home is also the same. While it is polygamous giving children a limited chance to develop themselves, it is clear that Uncle Simiren is the authority in the home.

Ole Kulet makes it clear that culture and tradition are culpable in not only justifying male treatment of women in this society but also in making women submissive to them. While Mama Milanoi is naïve about her station in life, Simiren's wives are actually happy and proud of the station their society endows on them. Though FGM abuses them, they embrace it and ironically have a similar attitude to it as the menfolk in their society. The same is seen for Nabaru, Olarinkoi's mother as well as the three young women Resian meets while living at Olarinkoi's home. The biggest point about this thinking is made through the fact that the said women do not only fail to question female circumcision but they also appear proud of it regardless of the fact that it is shown to be pointless and a means of making women subservient. The author, for example, uses Oloisudori's insistence on FGM to show that it is men in the society who use it to make women submissive meaning that Nabaru and Olarinkoi's mother praise it because of the shame they have for having submitted to it. They therefore punish young girls because they were themselves punished as is so clear in Olarinkoi's sarcastic remarks and mocking laughter to Resian; there is nothing dignified in her insistence on the ritual. It appears she would get vicarious pleasure through Resian's pain. Through them, the author suggests that women are their own enemies. Olarinkoi's mother, Simiren's wives and even Nabaru support FGM without questioning its veracity. With changes of attitude such as the one of Nabaru, the author suggests that the future is bright; this brightness however only comes with a rational examination of one's beliefs and values the way Nabaru does. Nabaru is properly put through this examination by Minik and the Kaelo girls until she sees their rationale and adopts their point of view.

Since it is a tool of submission, resisting FGM then becomes a big symbol of women emancipation. It is notable that the free women in this society must resist undergoing the rite whether it is for themselves or for other young women. Emakererei stands out in this regard. She does not only campaign against FGM but she has personally been liberated through education and a good enviable career. She also has her own home and therefore, no man can give her commands. For Resian, Ole Kaelo tries to use the right to establish his authority. This authority means forcing her to get circumcised, then marrying her off to a man of his choice. It follows therefore that resistance to one aspect of subservience is symbolic of resistance and rebellion to all. When

Resian refuses to get married off, she also resists getting circumcised which is a prerequisite to the marriage.

Seen from this perspective therefore, the author creates a crop of women who question the station given to the woman by culture and tradition. The best example comes in Minik ene Nkoitoi who is militant about girl circumcision and rescues young girls from both FGM and underage marriages. She creates a home which comes to symbolize a heavenly bliss to which any woman made submissive by culture can run to. Mink campaigns against the obnoxious traditions single-handedly. Through her, the author discusses the role of economic empowerment of women in the attempt to stop intolerable traditions. One reason why Mink is able to do what she does is because she is independent; this independence comes with her good education, her career as well as good job which allows her this independence and makes men dependent on her. This symbolically means that for all women to escape these traditions, they have to begin by acquiring education first. They have to follow this with good jobs or businesses that make them independent. Young girls such as the Kaelo daughters and the school children in her school are encouraged that they too can make it; it is the reason why their point of view is quite different compared with the three young women who Resian meets at Olarinkoi's place. The fact that they are young also suggests that the future is in good hands. The narrative ending with the Kaelo daughters going to college and therefore fulfilling their life ambition makes a big point on the likely future of young girls and the death of obnoxious traditions such as early marriage and FGM.

The author makes another point about the future of the girl child. Resian becomes a symbol of rebellion not only to her authoritative father but also to the society. She runs away from home to escape forced marriage and FGM. Her standing up to Ole Kaelo shows that all girls facing similar situations have an option because the first step becomes the symbolic rebellion to those families and societies which makes girls acquiescent.

Taiyo on the other hand becomes a symbol of hope for girls who have already been forced to undergo circumcision. She picks up her life even after she is circumcised and goes to college meaning that FGM is not the end of life. As harrowing as the rite might be, Ole Kulet suggests that women who have fallen victim have to accept themselves and move on. Her promise to stop the same happening to others especially her children symbolizes the fact that women who have learnt the lesson the hard way have to make a sacrifice; they have to ensure that they do not suffer in vain by making sure that what happens to them doesn't happen to others.

Greed and Materialism

This refers to the belief in wealth for its own sake to a point where individuals worship material things to the detriment of human values and feeling. Ole Kulet discusses how the lure of material things can corrode human values and make human beings robotic. It is suggested that human beings have to guard against this vice for it creeps into their lives slowly and changes their values. Ole Kaelo's life gives the reader a good insight into this. He starts well as a hardworking man intent on taking good care of his family. He isn't very interested in material possessions, fame or leadership which he leaves to his younger brother. His belief in material things and his leaning to cultural traditions however slowly changes him so that he becomes insensitive to the feelings of others. When he marries Mama Milanoi, for example, it appears that he genuinely loves her and wants nothing else short of her happiness and that of her children. His working for Ole Supeyo however makes him covet wealth and when he is retrenched, he tries all means necessary to acquire material wealth like other rich men. This makes him insensitive to his wife and children. He is insensitive to his wife's opinions and quite callous to the aspirations of his children. He silences his wife with intimidation and procrastinates about his daughters' intention to join the university so as to buy time. In the meantime, he gets naively caught up in Oloisudori's web and he is forced to make his daughters the sacrificial lambs.

Ole Kulet shows that Ole Kaelo's case isn't predetermined and therefore, it isn't exactly about adherence to culture and traditions as it were. While Ole Kaelo procrastinates about taking his children to college, it is clear that his visit to Oloisudori's home plays a big part in convincing him – or in making him rationalize – that he is doing the best for his daughter. This way, he puts material things before the welfare of his daughter. He is also eaten up by guilt about marrying his daughter to his age mate meaning that he isn't exactly convinced about early marriage and adherence to culture. He admires Ole Supeyo from an early age and takes him as his mentor. This leaves him susceptible to Oloisudori's extortion for his desires to get rich leaves him looking for quick ways of doing so. When Oloisudori offers him a chance, he does not stop to think twice. Through him, the author shows how coveting material gain can actually leave somebody worse than they were in the beginning. His wife is similarly lured by material things to connive with her husband in marrying Resian off. She is awed by both Oloisudori's home and the vehicle offered to take the couple home. She is as guilty as her husband as witness her tossing in bed all night as the thoughts of giving her daughter away instead of letting her make the decision eat at her conscience.

Oloisudori is however the best example of greed and materialism. He does not stop at anything to get rich including robbing, poaching and extortion. He flashes his wealth about and believes it is enough to endear him to other people, especially his wives. He travels in an entourage of vehicles, wears flashy clothes and jewelry to intimidate people into fearing him. This makes it easier for him to get his way around. The worst of him comes out in his attempt to marry Resian by force, first by influencing the parents followed by his extortion. He has no qualms about the age of the girl or the disruption of her life as a result of his cruel intentions. He is so assured of his self-importance that when Resian declines his hand, he laughs at her telling her that she is his wife whether she likes it or not. When she runs away to the Emakererei, he follows her and tries to intimidate Minik through his flashy cars and then threats. Minik's facing up to him becomes an important symbol of the need for all to fight materialism and stem its corrosion of society. The fact that Kaelo's girls aren't cowed by Oloisudori and neither are they lured into immorality by his money suggests the changing values of the new generation. Ole Kaelo suggests therefore that there is still hope. The girls prefer to improve themselves through education rather than cling to Oloisudori's wealth.

Culture and Tradition

This has been a controversial question through time the world over. While people have genuine ways why they come up with certain values to steer them through life, it becomes pointless to follow some customs if they are regressive or if they are no longer useful to society. Ole kulet doesn't directly criticize such retrogressive customs. Knowing the sensitivity with which such customs are held, he chooses an indirect approach.

His biggest criticism is levelled on FGM. It is seen as retrogressive not only in the way it is used as an excuse to prepare girls for early marriage but more importantly because, despite the pain, embarrassment and the health risks it puts its victims through, it doesn't add any value to those who undergo it. What is worse is that they are forced into it without any genuine reason. He shows that with time, certain customs become the norm and create fear in people especially if the origins are unclear. People are afraid of criticizing them because they feel they will be ostracized. They therefore follow them blindly and are forced to live with more retrogressive, sometimes health-threatening issues rather than criticize what they do not understand. In the society of the novel, for example, women go through FGM, even embrace it for fear of going against social custom, though they agree that the custom is purposeless. Nabaru for instance agrees that FGM is backward and purposeless. It appears therefore that the reason she has always supported it is because she is afraid of going against the grain.

Some who campaign for it have other selfish reasons. Olarinkoi's mother supports it because she belongs to dying tradition herself. Her relevance to society can only be seen in terms of her prophesies – prophesies which aren't materializing – and therefore, she has to support any other customs that go in line with beliefs in tradition, superstition and the determination of the progress of life by the unnatural. Girl abduction and early marriage are part of this custom and therefore, she supports them too in an attempt to get her son a wife. It is no wonder therefore that Resian's abduction goes hand in hand with circumcision and traditional medicine which makes the likes of the *enkabaani* relevant in their society. When Nabaru visits the sheep farm, she witnesses the strength of modern medicine and has to accept that FGM is a dying custom. Oloisudori on the other hand uses the practice to make his abduction and forced marriage of Resian a possibility. While he is an incorrigible criminal, he knows he cannot hide if he abducts the girl; if it is done under the guise of traditions, however, no one is likely to question it. In fact, many people will support him. His use of material things to lure both the girls and their parents however suggests that what he is thinking about is self-interest and not culture or tradition.

Ole Kaelo is treated in the same way. He starts out to first make himself rich but when his foolish naiveté lands him in Oloisudori's tentacles, he tries to fall back on culture so as to rationalize the marriage of his daughter – which is in fact a cover-up for being rescued by Oloisudori out of his economic mire. This proves that his retreat to Nasila, his homecoming and his attempt to fall back on culture all have to do with his foolish mistakes in business and therefore, he offers his children as scapegoats to cover this. It is clear too that Ole Kaelo isn't an ardent believer in either culture or tradition in that though tradition gives him the position of head of the family, he isn't interested and lets his younger brother Simiren steer the Kaelo family. When he comes to try and reclaim that position in his middle age, his reasons for doing so definitely become suspect.

Ole Kulet shows the inevitability of the death of such customs by exposing the hypocrisy behind them. While some people use such to get themselves beautiful girls as wives without the girls' consent, others lean on culture to feed their lust for many wives and to bury the problems of inability to rear and educate the children resulting from such polygamous marriages. The bulk of them however find themselves in such a quagmire because they are afraid to question the relevance of what they do for fear of being branded anti-community. Pursuit of a boy child may be one reason that can lead a man who is culturally conscious to have too many children. Ole Kulet shows that such idiosyncrasies have their day of reckoning. There is a tidal wave coming and there is little people can do to stop it. This is largely suggested by the success of the Emakererei, Resian and Taiyo's win over their parents as well as the wave of education sweeping through the land. Girls are becoming self-determining and economically powerful and this goes a long way in accepting and maintaining the new status quo.

Ole Kulet also criticizes early marriage as an institution in society. While it is shown to be cruel in the way girls who get married this way lack rights of their own, it also kills the dreams of many. We meet many young women in the narrative whose dreams come to a drastic end because some man somewhere decides for them that it is time to get married. Ole Kulet criticizes the objectification of such women because the dowry paid to their fathers for them becomes what sends their dreams to their death bed. This is well symbolized in Resian's escape and the spirited hunt for her by Oloisudori who argues that he has already paid dowry for her and therefore, her marriage to him is a foregone conclusion. Ole kulet shows that even FGM becomes a necessary rationalization that leads to early marriage; the hypocritical few who want a second wife quote culture. When they do so, they must invariably quote FGM as a preparation of a woman for marriage. This way, the two types of outdated rituals are maintained. It would therefore mean that the death of one would lead to the effective death of the other. Girls who haven't undergone FGM choose their own way to get married, therefore they are unlikely to become statistics of early marriages. Men who do not circumcise their girls will also find it difficult to quote culture should they want to marry a young girl without her consent.

Culture is thus seen to be a concept that is controversial. People cannot define exactly what it constitutes of. This vagueness is seen to give it a leeway for misuse because, unless the law comes out clearly to say what is right and what is wrong, there are many knaves who will continue to be egotistical, infringe on the rights of others and generally break the law and blame culture for it.

Betrayal

Ole Kulet deals with several levels of betrayal. Betrayal is seen as the backtracking from supporting positive values, whether they are personal, interpersonal or communal, largely as a result of self-interest and hypocritical narcissism.

Taiyo, for example betrays her sister when she refuses to support her opinions knowing very well that her sister is right. She takes the side of her parents or relatives because she wants to please them but secretly agrees with her sister. When Resian says that men should act responsibly, Taiyo knows the truth of it especially after being confronted on the second day after arriving at Nasila and considering the nature of her father. However, she believes that going against her parents' decisions is wrong and therefore chooses to criticize Resian. This is one reason which makes it easier for her parents' insensitivity to grow.

Mama Milanoi betrays her children in the same way. Her being naivety as a housewife denies her equal share in decision-making with her husband meaning that Ole Kaelo largely gets his way. This is also emphasized by her inability to get economic empowerment which leaves her and her children at the mercy of her husband. Similarly, she is blinded to her husband's intention in moving to Nasila and in setting up a business. The fact that she doesn't care where her husband's funds come from only seeing her prospects in good sons-in-law leaves her daughters open to exploitation. This gets worse when, like her husband, she begins rationalizing her daughter's marriage turning a blind eye to Resian ambition in education and career. She also turns a blind eye to the nature of Oloisudori though she feels guilty that she isn't doing the right thing. Ole Kulet shows that her indecision largely results from her lack of economic empowerment, the reason why her children have to seek this first if they are going to live any different from her.

Ole Kaelo betrays his daughters first in getting Taiyo circumcised against her will and second in trying to marry off Resian and thus forcing her to run away. He is easily to blame for all what his daughters go through. He pretends that he is 'going back to his people' through a sham homecoming ceremony knowing very well that it is a façade meant to rationalize his marrying off his daughter and get rescued out his business quagmire. The hypocrisy of the ceremony is seen in that he has to pay young men to organize it, rather than let them act out of their own volition if culture and tradition are the main point. This way, he is seen to commercialize culture so that it can serve his own end. He betrays his wife's love for her children in denying her any opinion about what happens to her daughters and in forcing her to go along with him in trying to get them circumcised and married off. He also disregards the feelings of his children. He denies them the right to further education and tries to determine their lives against their will.

Oloisudori betrays his society in many ways. He steals from one and all then extorts money and favors from people around him. He poaches elephant tusks and rhinoceros horns to enrich himself. He lures people into his traps and takes advantage of children denying them the right to education, proper marriage, self-determination and general pursuit of happiness.

Through such characters, Ole Kulet discusses the need for the society to reevaluate its values. He shows how worship of material things has made parents to betray their children and people to betray their country. People have resorted to the pursuit of personal happiness irrespective of its effect another and on national good. This way, he suggests the need to reevaluate social values and for people to commit themselves to the betterment of society like Mink, which he sees as the essence of personal happiness.

Children and Family

One of Ole Kulet's basic concerns is how parents treat their children, what right they have for doing so and, where it is wrong, what can be done about it. This is pitted against the various form of societies that he depicts in his novel. There are modern societies which are governed by law but there are others where the law is not as effective, and where people are a little shy to apply it because of the traditional nature of those societies.

Through the Kaelo family, Ole kulet portrays a modern society which believes in work, education and the right of the individual. Contrasted to Simiren's family which is polygamous and where the wives and the children do not question the patriarch, the behavior of each family is quite unique. Ole Kaelo's daughters are educated and with education comes the knowledge – and the right – to question the status quo. Taiyo and Resian question both the way their father behaves as well as the docile nature of their aunts in a family where men idle and expect women to work for them. The docility of the woman in such a set-up is emphasized by Yeiyo-botorr's argument in favor of her own perdition. This means that the values of each family are quite different. Simiren's children also present a pathetic picture. They are many and unkempt, comparing them to their cousins. Even so, Simiren's wives continue giving birth as witness the two women who are pregnant when Ole Kaelo's girls visit them.

Ole Kulet however suggests that, without the use of effective law, people are bound to take advantage of such a setup. When Ole Kaelo realizes that he cannot command his children around, he falls back on tradition to as to have protection for his hypocrisy. He tries to educate his daughters about tradition so as to have them readily accept circumcision and being married off. This however clashes with his daughters' already held values so that rather than submit to their father's tyranny, they choose to rebel and run away. This way, Ole Kulet shows that unlike popular belief, not all parents have positive intentions for their children. In fact, outsiders like Minik ene Nkoitoi may have the welfare of the children at heart while their parents do not. It is quite ironical that Ole Supeyo chances her away in order to have the chance to violet the rights of his girls. Ole Kulet shows that in many circumstances, the government may need to put its foot down in order to keep predatory parents in check – especially those who think of their children as their property.

Against the background abuse of children's' rights comes Minik ene Nkoitoi. She realizes that in a society such as hers, there is a need to stand up against some issues and establish a haven where children who suffer from culturally determined problems can run to. She therefore becomes the only voice for children exploited both by culture and by their families. This way, Ole Kulet criticizes the government's blind eye to cultural exploitation and seeing that change might take time to come by, suggests the need for philanthropic people like Minik to intervene. Ole Kulet also suggests that children's rights are often curtailed without their knowledge (sometimes even by a well-meaning parents or society) but where children feel the need to change this, they should be bold enough to stand up against exploitation. Ole Supeyo and Simiren appear well-meaning enough in the way they bring up their children but it is clear that in such societies, there are hyenas who will come to take advantage of the situation. Oloisudori becomes the best symbol of those who fall back on tradition because it allows them to exploit the weak. His wealth is criminally acquired and it is suggested that even in Nakuru, the government is either incapable or unwilling to bring him to book. In such circumstances therefore, it is left for the victims such as Resian and to people such as Minik to stand up against such brutality.

Education and Career

In *Blossoms of the Savannah*, the position of the woman is largely seen to result from her denial of education and the resultant lack of empowerment because of the careers she finds herself in. Even in a modern family such as Kaelo's, Mama Milanoi becomes submissive because she is uneducated and therefore ends up a housewife to a man who is not only the breadwinner in the family but one who is patriarchal and authoritative. The wives of Simiren are actually worse. While their work is to cook and look after their children, they have little say as regards how many children they can have or even what direction the lives of their children should take. Ole Kulet shows that some of these circumstances are deliberately upheld so as to maintain men in a certain position. Oloisudori marries many women and their test to become married is determined by him. This means therefore that they become dependent on and subservient to him afterwards. They have no say as to their own self-improvement or about who else is married to the home. So that his authority remains unquestioned, Oloisudori uses the patriarchal position given him by tradition and culture. This is one reason why he has his wives circumcised because in his other spheres of life, it is quite obvious that he cares little for culture or the upholding of human values which culture seeks to maintain.

Ole Kulet argues that this status quo can only be changed by women standing up to this exploitation. This can only happen if they are empowered through education and stopping the obnoxious practices such as circumcision which are meant to maintain their subservience, and which are one means of denying girls the empowerment they get through education. This is seen in that women who have dared rise against these circumstances are seen to be independent. Minik, for example, lives a carefree life with no one determining her self-worth or even self-improvement. She is well educated and the fact that she has gone as far as Makerere serves as a big warning to anyone who might want to mess with her. In fact, one reason why she is taunted as Emakererei is because it is assumed that her ideas about stopping FGM emanate from her having gone to Makerere University. This way, Makerere University itself, as an epitome of learning, becomes a big symbol of empowerment and rebellion for women who want to change the status quo. Through the image of Minik, the university also symbolizes emancipation through modern careers – and so do other educational institutions such as Egerton University.

Ole kulet also suggests that the reason why many men want girls circumcised is for their own egoistic reasons. Ole Supeyo, for example, is polygamous. To ensure his security in polygamy, he looks down on women including his own daughters. He educates all his sons, including sending some to the university, while he denies the same to his daughters. Apparently, his reason stems from the fact that girls are only fit for marrying off – like he marries them himself – and that polygamy is quite alright. He argues too that to remain in polygamous marriages, women need to be tamed through circumcision. This essentially means that he circumcises his daughters, denies them education and marries them off so as to rationalize his own polygamy. When Mink comes to try to make him stop circumcising his daughters, it is revealed that his attitude towards women will not let him do so. He sees women as wild animals that must be tamed the way a cow needs to be dehorned. Education itself must be used to educate such ignorant people so they can change their attitude the way Nabaru does.

Minik becomes a great inspiration to young girls because of her independence and her illustrious career. She commands a sheep farm many thousands of acres large and puts up a school where rescued girls get education. This is one reason why Resian and her sister are attracted to her. Through this, Ole Kulet shows that women need somebody among them not only to fight for their cause but also to inspire young girls to develop themselves. Minik is also seen as a light among the women. Her education lets her see not only the pointlessness of some customs but also the real reason some men insist on maintaining them. It is through her that the likes of Nabaru come to see that FGM is wrong and change their attitude towards it. This suggests that education plays a big role in educating the women and removing their ignorance. This way, education serves a big role in stopping obnoxious customs and in empowering women to build strong careers.

Town versus Country

The novel also draws a contrast between town and country in terms of how people live and what they believe. Nakuru town is as an image of progress and an epitome of positive change. Firstly, the Kaelos are a happy family when they live in Nakuru town. There is little conflict between the children who symbolize the future and the parents who symbolize the past. Resian and Taiyo are optimistic about their going to university and Taiyo even has a boyfriend. For Resian, the only thing they are waiting for is their father's ok about their going to university. The children appear happy in Nakuru and the town and its surrounding appears ok and secure, if not protective of them. Ole Kaelo and his wife are independent in thought and this is one thing that makes them respect their daughters' wishes.

When the family moves to the countryside, the parents are influenced by their neighbors and especially the Simiren family. Ole Kaelo now wants to take over as the leader of the family as tradition requires. He also wants to be integrated properly into the Nasila culture and one way of doing so is having their daughters circumcised. Though Ole Kaelo might have other reasons for moving to the country and wanting to embrace the Nasila culture, his movement to the countryside becomes a big determinant of his behavior and so does it do to his wife's decisions. In Nakuru, Mama Milanoi isn't very worried what will become of her daughters but after they move to Nasila, she begins thinking that her relevance in this community will be determined by her daughters marrying into the right families. This way, the country becomes not only a symbol of retrogression but it also curtails the freedom of the young in terms of thought and advancement.

Nasila also becomes a symbol of lack of freedom for the young - physical and mental - and the former emphasizes the latter. Taiyo and Resian are attacked immediately they go to Nasila. For some time, they are even hidden at their uncle's home. Resian's flight later is also symbolic of running away from this insecurity and so is her sister's rescue later. In Nakuru too, the girls have a better chance of convincing their father about their going to university because even Kaelo's mind is open. When they move to Nasila however, both the curtailing of physical movement and the immersion into cultural tradition becomes symbolic of the limited choice the girls have. Their enjoying nature and the open country, while being contrasted to their looking out from the window of their bedroom in Nakuru, ironically comes to stand for retardation in thinking and the limiting of choice. This way, Ole Kulet suggests that children have better freedom and chances of success in town than in the countryside. It also means that parents become more close minded in the country than in town. This in itself means that backward traditions are likely to be rifer in the country. While the town therefore becomes symbolic of physical and mental advancement, the country symbolizes retardation and cultural backwardness.

The author also discusses other sub-themes which you can develop on your own. He discusses **retirement** and what people ought to do or not to do about it. It is seen that making preparations for retirement may not be enough in itself; many people lose their retirement benefits because of ill-planning. Ole Kulet also suggests that those who retire are naïve and are likely to fall prey to knaves as they try to invest their lifesavings. Should they invest in business like Ole Kaelo does, there they find practiced businessmen whose rule of the thumb is ruthless competition including taking advantage of the guileless in the name of thrift. Thus, any retiree needs to be wary of the nature of the society into which s/he retires.

Change is discussed too. Many people appear resistant to change especially in cases where change is disadvantageous to them. The men in the Nasila society are averse to change because it is seen to deny them some benefits. Ole Kulet however shows that change is a tide that will carry away anyone who stands in its way; it carries Ole Kaelo and Oloisudori with it. **Generational conflict/gap** is discussed through the contrast of the girls to their parents and their aunts. This emphasizes the incongruity of their thinking showing one reason why the youth and their parents cannot see eye to eye. Other subthemes you might want to consider include **Hypocrisy and Pretense, Love** (both passionate and filial), **Religion and Superstition.**

THE ELEMENTS OF STYLE

Style is a mode of undertaking certain tasks. It is that distinctive way of going about things or activities that makes one a unique individual. Sometimes it is as personal as your handwriting which cannot be similar even for identical twins because for handwriting, style may be as unique as one's way of shaping the letters which would make your handwriting recognizable to people used to it even if you tried to change it. Style is acquired over time. In literature, style refers to an author's manner of writing through the specific use of language, treatment of characters and themes which makes us familiar with the author so much that if we took another work by the same author, we can recognize their hand in it even before we know that the work is theirs. It is however important to recognize the fact that all authors have specific elements of style at their disposal. These include characterization, symbolism, irony, personification and the like. What they do with these elements of style to create unique works of art becomes their style. It is therefore important to study these elements of style carefully before embarking on an examination of a novel's or author's style. (The last part of this book gives you the possible elements of style in a novel. Study them carefully before you continue).

Let us consider some important elements of style in *Blossoms of the Savannah*.

The Title

Titles are often important in novels because they help the reader unravel what the story is about. It is important to note however that, titles require proper consideration because while some are obvious in reference, others may be symbolic, ironic or even downright satirical. It is also possible for the reader to see a lot more than what is meant, meaning that titles can be misinterpreted.

Ole Kulet's title, Blossoms of the Savannah, has a number of suggestions. Firstly, blossoms are flowers and therefore, the title connotes beauty, physical or symbolic. If you have visited a savannah grassland, say, in Maasailand or Samburu after the rains (sometimes even shortly before) you may have noticed how flowering plants begin to have a flowery twinge in anticipation of the rain or as a result of it. This 'blossoming' leaves such country beautiful to look at (not to mention the scent of the many flowers). Taken this way, the title suggests the beauty of the savannah at the blossoming time because this is the time that this country is most beautiful, most productive. Thinking of the savannah from the point of its sere nature especially before it blossoms, then the savannah itself maybe symbolic of a country that is in want. This way, the blossoms of the savannah become quite significant in suggesting the best time for the savannah in terms of its beauty and productivity and in connoting the continuation of life.

On the other hand, this meaning can be extended in the fact that the title is symbolic. The blossoms here are those who dare (just like savannah blossoms dare a harsh environment) and those who come to fruition like savannah flowers. This way, the title suggests people like Minik ene Nkoitoi who live in a difficult environment, but who dare to change it and to blossom themselves, and as a result, they gain the most from this harsh environment. Those plants that blossom into flower in the savannah are the hope of the vegetation of the next season. Minik becomes the hope of the woman of the next generation through her daring fight against FGM and early marriages.

Also, these flowering blossoms may be seen in terms of not only their anticipation but also in their suggestion of the new season; the more the blossoms, the better the next season is likely to be. Resian and Taiyo blossom into the flowers of the next season in that while both go to the university and becomes symbols of the next generation of Mink ene Nkoitoi, Resian's militant rebellion suggests an even better generation, the reason why Minik admires her, while Taiyo is symbolic of a change in attitude for those girls who have already fallen victim to FGM. They are down but not out. These blossoms are also suggested in that Resian and Taiyo do not blossom in Nakuru town, though it looks quite likely they would. Ole Kulet has them travel to the savannah country of Nasila where they blossom by going to university because their example is required here more than in Nakuru. They bring their rebellious blossoming to girls who would have been content to grow in cultural exploitation. For Resian, it is the three young women she meets who have already been married too early. For the two girls, it is the young girls at the Ntare-Naaju school who watch them resist Oloisudori and go to Egerton University. These young girls in this school are blossoms in themselves considering the fact that the challenge thrown to them by Resian and Taiyo is likely to see them do a lot bigger things than the two girls. Like the flowers that blossom in the sere savannah therefore, these young girls blossom despite the harsh conditions they have suffered where they've been rescued from and despite their being excommunicated by their families. This way, the title suggests that despite the savannah being a harsh environment, it is probably the best breeding ground for flowers that will withstand the test of time; thus it may not be a wonder if Ole Musanka's prediction of the next leader of Maa coming from the Taiyo generation, literally or literary.

The Setting

In any narrative, the setting becomes important in terms of both space and time because the veracity of a narrative can only be determined by a consideration of events against their setting. *Blossoms of the Savannah* largely relies on two settings; the countryside of Nasila, a back-of-beyond rural town in the heart of Maa country, and Nakuru, a modern town in the heart of the Rift Valley. Nakuru is important in giving the narrative a space and geographical location because it tells us that we are dealing with events in Kenya, a country in Africa. This evokes thoughts of socio-cultural change as can be seen in many narratives that have used the town versus country motif, a good example being Peter Abrahams *Mine Boy*. Therefore, we expect the Kaelo family to be 'modern' in thought and behavior and this becomes crucial as we examine Ole Kaelo's motives in moving to the countryside. Nasila on the other hand becomes important because it evokes thoughts of countryside ignorance at best and rural naiveté at worst. This not only explains the thoughts and behavior of the populace in Nasila but it also puts to question the motives of urbanites such as Oloisudori and Ole Kaelo in moving to Nasila and exploiting its cultural beliefs.

The town-and-country setting therefore becomes important in establishing a basis for the town versus country conflict as well as that of the characters thinking of what Resian and Taiyo believe in and how they behave seen against the beliefs and behavior of Nasila community.

It should be noted that Ole Kulet avoids specific commitment in terms socio-historic setting of the narrative. Though we know that the narrative is set among the Maa, Ole Kulet does not give it a historical time. This is because societies change through history and therefore, an evocation of a specific historical time would mean that the cultural settings would have to be seen against that specific time. By being deliberately vague, Ole Kulet gives his narrative a timelessness so that it is relevant to many situations, historical times as well as cultural settings. This does not however deny it its flavor of the Maa culture which is crucial for the Maa have been seen as one community that has withstood the test of time in terms of cultural change.

Point of View

The novel largely uses the third person point of view. The story is narrated by an **omniscient narrator** who is able to get into and out of characters. This is crucial not only in relating events which happen in many places but also in creating multi-faceted characters. This is one way in which the verisimilitude of the characters becomes easily possible while giving them depth of character and opinion.

The **third person** is if course, spiced up with dialogue in which characters are allowed to voice personal opinions especially those that may be difficult to present from another point of view. Resian's attitude to Oloisudori makes sound sense when she is made to sound it herself when she discusses him with her sister. We are able to see a young girl's perception of an adult monstrosity both in term of Oloisudori, the monster, and in terms of a child considering marriage to an old man, an issue which belongs to the adult world. This way, we are made to feel how the adult world of her father and Oloisudori comes into sharp conflict with the innocent world of Resian the child and thereby violates it.

The narrative uses **authorial intrusion**. On pg. 168, for example, the narrative is forecasted through point of view in a way that the reader feels that this is a new point of view. This also happens on Pgs. 197 and 211. The intervention of the new point of view creates suspense as well as irony in that the reader is taken ahead of the narrative in learning of events at the expense of the characters who play them, creating situational irony as we watch characters get into situations they aren't prepared for while we are.

Personal reminisces are important too. They form a crucial third person limited point of view in personalizing the narrative at specific points. Through the thoughts of Mama Milanoi for example, we learn of her docility and submission. Through the same, we learn of Ole Kaelo's rationalization of his actions, thus see through his hypocrisy and pretense. This becomes more effective than it would were we to learn through the omniscient narrator.

Symbolism and Imagery

The richness of *Blossoms of the savannah* largely comes from its exploitation of rich imagery and the fact that many characters and events are symbolic. This allows Ole Kulet to tell in a few pages, a story that might have otherwise taken the length of the bible to relate.

Minik ene Nkoitoi is symbolic of the aspirations of many girls while her farm takes on the symbol of the heaven that girls in this society have been denied entry both in reality and in ideal. Minik does not only get well educated showing other girls what is possible but she also gets employed as a manager, a position where she is able to shift the focus of power from the male to the female. Her authoritative giving orders to men on her farm therefore becomes symbolic of the fact that education, which gives her this job, is the best tool for liberating young girls. It is quite apparent that without such education, Minik might have been as subservient in this society as any other woman. This way, her establishment of a school at Ntare-Naaju, her establishment of scholarships and her sending Resian and Taiyo to Egerton University become the best symbols of giving the young girls the kind of power and freedom that she enjoys.

Taiyo and Resian are themselves symbols. The way they struggle and their final emancipation speaks a lot about what is required in emancipating girls in real societies that practice early marriage and FGM. The fact that they are educated, know their rights and have aspirations to improve themselves by going to Egerton University says a lot about girls in worse circumstances. The pair are the last people we expect to be forced into either FGM or early marriage. The harrowing events they go through however emphasize the fact that no river is too wide or too deep to cross. Since they surmount such problems, it is symbolic of how much should be done to liberate girls in similar or worse circumstances. Their going to university in the end is symbolic of the blossoming of their dreams which is preparatory to their empowerment and changing the community the way Minik does. Their movement from Nakuru to Nasila is also symbolic of their 'exporting' their awareness to the rural communities and therefore comes to stand for what educated girls in towns should do for their counterparts in rural areas.

Oloisudori on the other hand is symbolic of male greed, chauvinism and immorality. He is quite incapable of putting himself in anyone else's shoes and is caricatured for his shortsightedness in being too full of himself as to think he can get everything he wants. He represents the extent to which materialism and greed can corrupt the society in his flashing his wealth about and expecting everyone to genuflect to him. In his insensitivity, he is compared to a monster whose only concern is what fills its belly. He symbolizes the evil in society which innocent young girls are faced with. What it takes to bring him down is also symbolic of the depth of work that waits to be done in order to liberate girls from FGM and early marriages.

Egerton University is symbolic of liberation from cultural slavery and obnoxious customs that bedevil the society. The fact that the two girls do not lose focus of their goal to get into Egerton University, the fact that they happily end up there shows that the university as a beacon of learning is symbolic of the heights girl children need to go to eradicate outdated customs meant to make them submissive. It is quite significant that the only woman who is able to stand up to cultural evil in the novel in one who has been to the university. It is also significant that the two girls who are rebellious against such customs also aim at getting into the university. This way, the university becomes a symbol of empowerment, female emancipation and enlightenment.

Many other symbols are used this way including the Kaelo's journey to Nasila which stands for retrogression, with the breaking down of the lorry symbolizing the time and chance the Kaelos are given to rethink. On pg. 117, water is used to symbolize Nasila culture. It is polluted by self-seekers meaning that Nasila culture is no longer reliable because self-seeking people misuse it to their own ends. The child who won't eat on pg. 19 and the older women on pg. 196 are also used symbolically in the same way.

Many images are also used to enhance the narrative. On pg. 7, Ole Kaelo uses the image of the baby to be born to capture the inevitability of retirement. Here, it is suggested that people need to accept that retirement will come one day and begin making preparations for it. On pg. 13, the elders liken Ole Kaelo to a mono-eyed giant standing on legs of straw. This image emphasizes Ole Kaelo's precarious nature in that he has no roots in his culture. The image shows Ole Kaelo's reckoning about his people which later leads him to seek reentry into the Nasila culture. In some way, it creates foreshadowing.

Many metaphors enrich the narrative too. On pg. 24, Ole Kaelo likens himself to a young bull in pasture and Ole Supeyo to an old one. He uses the images to emphasize his conviction about the veracity of his business ideas. This is quite ironic because later, it is Ole Supeyo who is proven right. A little later, he likens Ole Supeyo to a person who destroys a bridge once they've crossed it to deny others the chance to do so. This captures the sense that Ole Supeyo might be jealous of upcoming businessmen like Ole Kaelo. Kaelo is later proven wrong showing his shortsightedness and Ole Supeyo's open and trustworthy nature. Ole Supeyo himself likens Oloisudori to a hyena which shouldn't be allowed into a homestead. This emphasizes Oloisudori's treachery. When the advice isn't taken, this shows Kaelo's shortsightedness and forecasts his doom so that we have little pity for him when his daughters run away. Other striking metaphors are used on pages 174, 192, 197, and 205. Examine them on your own to see their suitability in context.

Similes are used too. On pg. 170, Ole Kaelo's cowardice and intimidation is captured in his comparison to a tortoise withdrawing into its shell. This shows Ole Kaelo's insensitivity and hypocrisy in avoiding the confrontation with his daughter. On pg. 171, Resian likens Oloisudori to a monster. This stresses her dislike for him and emphasizes his intimidation to her. When Ole Kaelo insists on his way therefore, we see his insensitivity to his daughter and his meanness and egotistical nature in forcing her to undergo the encounter with Oloisudori so that he can benefit. On pg. 176, Kaelo's greed is captured in his tongue flicking out 'like that of a chameleon'. This shows how much he covets material possessions like Oloisudori's car. This foreshadows the narrative in that we know that he can do anything to get riches, including selling off his daughters at the prime time of going to the university. Other good similes are used on pgs. 192, 194, 210, and 215. Examine these and others in the light of what they add to the narrative.

Allusion

Ole Kulet uses a number of allusions in this novel. On pg. 23, Ole Kulet alludes to Luke 9: 62 in the words, '...he put his hand to the plough'. Here, Jesus emphasizes the need to serve God without focusing on any other thing. By using these words, Ole Kaelo suggest his determination in doing what he is about to start when he lands in Nasila. This suggests his industry while suggesting that he is shortsighted in that he doesn't consider other serious issues. When he is taken advantage of by Oloisudori we learn that it is necessary not only to be industrious and committed to your work but also to ensure that cunning people do not pull your food out of your mouth.

On pg. 27, the author alludes to the sword of Damocles, a literary allusion to the story given by Cicero in *Tusculan Disputations*. During the reign of King Dionysius II, Damocles flattered the king about his happy comfortable life and the king offered him his throne for a day – a throne which had a sharp sword hanging by a strand of horsehair above it. Noticing the sword, Damocles was so nervous as to ask the king to take back the throne. Cicero's moral was that there can never be any happiness with constant apprehensions. Used in context, this **literary allusion** stresses the fears the girls have to live with since there is a constant fear of attack from people who want to circumcise them.

On pg. 176, the author alludes to *A Major Domo* (sic) a **literary allusion** to *Under Major Domo Minor* by Patrick deWitt a story about serving the high and mighty. The allusion seems intended to emphasize the supplicating nature of Ole Kaelo to Oloisudori and thus emphasize how intimidated by the latter Ole Kaelo is. This is important in shining Ole Kaelo's character and in emphasizing his changing character in readiness for the bombshell of Resian's forced marriage and the resultant clashing conflict.

On pg. 185, the author alludes to **oral tradition** in the form of the legendary beautiful brown girl to which Oloisudori refers. The allusion is meant to trap Ole Kaelo since Oloisudori pretends that he is deeply in love with his daughter; the audience knows he only lusts for her. This is meant to be a softer landing for Ole Kaelo in committing himself to marrying his daughter to Oloisudori since we already know that he has been denied an alternative. Another similar allusion is done by Joseph Parmuat in the narrative of the Olarinkoi. It is meant to give root to the practice of FGM and show that women are indeed their own enemy for conniving to continue the tradition. Whether the narrative is real or a creation of Ole Kulet is a different matter.

On pgs. 186-7, a **historical allusion** is made to Lord Ngata (Lord Egerton). The true story is told of how the Lord built a beautiful castle for a woman he loved but his love was unrequited. This led Egerton to dislike women so much that no woman was ever allowed to grace that castle in his lifetime. The allusion emphasizes Oloisudori's lust for Resian while forecasting that his love will be unrequited. This helps in both exposition and in creating suspense

On pg. 194, a **political allusion** is made to the Goldenberg and Anglo-leasing scandals (sic) in Kenya's history which are alleged to have fleeced the public of millions of shillings. Ole Kaelo uses the allusion to rationalize his behavior. His guilt tells him that what he is doing in marrying off his daughter is wrong but he rationalizes that she is the 'fruit of his labor' just like those caught up in the said scandals claim the wealth they have is the fruit of their labor. The allusion emphasizes Ole Kaelo's guilt in his rationalizing his behavior while emphasizing his objectification of his daughter who is treated as fruits of his labor. Another **biblical allusion** is made on pgs. 229-30.

Language

It might be important to make one or two comments about the language and its effects. The author uses quite a number of idioms which spice up the language. On pg. 24, the idiom 'threw caution to the wind' stresses Ole Kaelo's carelessness in dismissing the wise counsel of his friend. This is important not only in building Ole Kaelo's character but also in forecasting his doom. On pg. 26 the idiom 'pour cold water on' emphasizes Ole Kaelo's disappointment in Ole Supeyo's reaction to his ideas. This shows that Ole Kaelo had not thought deeply about who he was dealing with and this underlines his naiveté. On pg. 185, the idiom 'the scales had fallen from his eyes' underscores the effect of material possessions on Ole Kaelo which helps in satirizing him. By the scales falling from his eyes, Ole Kaelo becomes more insensitive rather than more intelligent as it should be. On pg. 186, the idiom 'birds of the same feather' stresses the difference of Lord Ngata and his beloved, emphasizing the former's naivety. The contrast helps stress the similarity between the Lord and Oloisudori and thus Oloisudori's insensitivity and gullibility. Many other idioms are used.

Freudian slips are also used to reveal Ole Kaelo's character. First, Ole Kaelo reveals to Ole Supeyo that he is about to sign four-year contracts. This demonstrates his hasty ineptitude in business in his revealing business secrets. On the other hand, this demonstrates his inexperience and therefore forecasts his doom in his relationship with the more experienced, more cunning Oloisudori. Ole Kaelo also reveals his meeting with Oloisudori which has a similar effect in revealing his stupidly too-trusting nature.

On pg. 194, the narrative uses **euphemism**. The term 'fruits of their labor' is meant to make theft look positive by clouding the means through which riches are acquired.

Foreshadowing

Blossoms of the Savannah is replete with foreshadowing. On pg. 3, Resian's talking about the success of the shop forecasts the narrative. Apart from the fact that the reader begins trying to get clues as to whether this will happen or not, what she says suggests that their father is not ready to move to Nasila or he is too hasty. When his business actually collapses later, we are forced to regard Resian and her father in a different light. While we see the father's hasty nature, we also recognize Resian's intuition and intelligence. On pg. 18, the confrontation of the young man and the girls speaks of worse things to come. While it suggests the real depth of danger the girls are in, it forecasts the second attack and the girl's final disappearance. This is further emphasized by the young man's words, 'You have not seen the last of me'. Pg. 19. On pg. 26, Ole Supeyo's advice to Kaelo to keep Oloisudori away from his daughters is foreshadowing. It forecasts not only Oloisudori's character as a lustful unrelenting bully but it also suggests that the attack on the girls and their being forced into marriage is inevitable.

Ole Kaelo's ominous silence on pg. 27 is foreshadowing. It suggests that there is more to the family's future than meets the eye. This is emphasized by Ole Kaelo's falling back as his family goes eagerly to the new house; the fact that he built it but he is hesitant suggests that he is guilty and unsure about the means through which it was built casting a shadow on the family's enjoyment of the house in the future. This way, Oloisudori's demands hardly come as a surprise. On pg. 214, the driver's reference to Resian as 'woman' foreshadows Olarinkoi's attempted rape. The fact that he regards her as a woman, not as a girl suggests that the driver knows a lot more – he is probably in the know about Olarinkoi's intentions. It comes as little surprise therefore when first, the driver 'dumps' them at Olarinkoi's gate and later when Olarinkoi tries to rape her and treats her like his wife. There are many other examples of foreshadowing in the narrative.

Motifs

Several motifs are used too. **Song** is used as a motif to suggest celebration or to capture people's aspirations. The song of the three blind mice captures Taiyo's aspirations to be like the Emakererei. She would want to punish those women who work hand in hand with men to exploit women. However, her powerlessness at this point is captured in her criticism of the three types of women through the song in which they are symbolized by blind mice. The song on pg. 186 captures the aspirations of the morans in convincing the brown girl to love them. The song on pg. 186 captures the aspirations of the children in the primary school and symbolically all other progressive girls. This way, the daughters of Maa refers to all girls who want to fight outdated customs, get educated and change the future of their community.

Journey is also a significant motif. Journey is seen as changing the lives of characters in significant ways. Four journeys standout in the narrative. The first journey is that of the Kaelo family to Nasila. This journey symbolizes retrogression in that the family moves from a comfortable town to an insecure countryside where almost everyone has something to fear. The second journey is that of Ole Kaelo and his wife to Nakuru town where they visit Oloisudori's home. When they return, they are changed people; they are ready to sell off their daughter with no qualms as to her opinion. Indeed, it is hardly possible to associate the parents who go to Oloisudori's home with the ones that return. Resian's journey as she escapes home is quite significant. It demonstrates her cutting ties with an oppressive past as well as symbolizing what other girls have to fight with to liberate themselves. Going to Ntare-Naaju is the crowning of this; her thought and outlook is completely changed so that now she can talk boldly and can manage herself as an adult. Lastly, the girls' journey to the university crowns them all. It is a fulfilment of the aspirations of the book itself and a symbol of the final emancipation. The fact that it is referred to every few pages makes it the turning point of the narrative. There are several other less significant journeys which should be examined in the same way.

One other motif is **dream**. On pg. 194, Ole Kaelo dreams that Resian has consented to marrying Oloisudori. The dream symbolizes the depth of conflict between the parents and the children. While the parents hope the dream will be fulfilled, the children are busy hatching a plan of a different kind. The dream also symbolizes the depth of guilt in the parents. Although they continue with the insistence on circumcision and marriage for their daughters, deep down inside, they know and feel that what they are doing is wrong. Resian herself dreams that the circumciser at Nasila, Olarinkoi's mother and Nabaru try to circumcise her. She attacks the circumciser vowing that she would never be a threat to another girl. The dream captures Resian's hopelessness while underlining women's culpability in being enemies of their own selves

Flashbacks

There are several flashbacks in the narrative. These come in form of characters' reminiscences of past events. They serve to fill in on the plot as well as give detail or hue to characters and events. On pg. 2, Taiyo flashes back to an incident in which her father denies her permission to attend a music extravaganza despite music being her best hobby. The flashback captures her father's authoritative nature. It also forecasts the oncoming clash between the father and the daughters. Pgs. 7-10 flash back on the life of Kaelo's family. It shines details of Kaelo's employment and retrenchment as well as Mama Milanoi's relationship with him since marriage. It shows Kaelo's attitude to his two daughters and of significance is that between him and Resian. It traces the root of the father's hate for his daughter and therefore forecasts the conflict between the two. On pg. 115, Mama Milanoi remembers a story from her youth in which a disrespectful old man is punished by women. This stresses how far women's power has been lost through time and therefore calls for the need to reexamine this. On pg. 153, Resian's mind flashes back to a childhood memory where their father had taken them to the Nakuru Agricultural Show. In the flashback, she remembers the docile white sheep. The flashback emphasizes her longing to meet Nkoitoi and stresses Resian's despondency. On pg. 272, Taiyo's mind flashes back to the day she goes to Esoit, the town her sister is reportedly hiding in. the flashback emphasizes the trauma caused by the harrowing incident of her circumcision. It reveals her betrayal by her own mother who lets her go without questioning the motives of the women who take her away. There are quite a number of other flashbacks and reminiscences.

Use of Rhetorical questions

Rhetorical questions are used on several occasions to echo ideas and suggest people's motive for action or behavior. They demonstrate the direction of characters' thoughts so that the decisions they make become obvious and justifiable to them. On pg. 24, it is used to emphasize Ole Kaelo's sense of pride as he questions Ole Supeyo's treatment of him. When he falls into Oloisudori's trap, the reader remembers him trying to justify his intelligence here. On pg. 27, this is followed by Ole Kaelo wondering through rhetoric questions again. Here, however, the questions prove that he has known the nature of Oloisudori all along; he tries to justify his doing business with him but his guilt still gnaws at his conscience. On pg. 192, rhetoric questions are used to emphasize the guilt of Mama Milanoi. Though it has already been agreed to marry off her daughter, she feels guilty for abetting her ensnarement and chicanery. On the following page, Ole Kaelo continues to rationalize Oloisudori's criminal activities. This is seen through the rhetoric questions that demonstrate his wondering and his justification so as to keep his conscience clear. Rhetoric questions are also used on pgs. , 205, 210, 217 and 19.

Irony and Sarcasm

Irony and sarcasm are used in various ways. Ole Kaelo's situation is ironical in several ways. To begin with, he works so hard, being quite shrewd, cunning and industrious according to his wife only to lose his life earnings in the very end to a crook who ensnares him like a child. It would appear that he grows more stupid as he ages rather than the other way round. The same is suggested by his reverting to the old traditional ways when he is old. It would be expected he'd show such ignorance in his youth but the irony is that he is not only old but time has also progressed so much that he'd be the last person we expect to revert to tradition. This however emphasizes that his need to go back to the old ways maybe suspect; it may be driven by hypocritical motives. Resian's cooking for Oloisudori is quite ironic.

Her parents know her abhorrence of the man and so ordering her to cook for him is tantamount to arranging for the poisoning of their prospective son-in-law. More ironical is the fact that even when her attitude to the man changes, they do not suspect her motives and therefore her turnabout and running away comes as quite a shock. Irony here emphasizes the parents' need to get Resian to agree to marry Oloisudori by all means necessary. It is also ironical that Oloisudori wants Resian to cook for them. This emphasizes his lust for her and his incapability of accepting that she hates him. This stresses his belief in himself and his ability to bring people round to his way of thinking using material things.

Situational irony is built when Resian is summoned by her father. She goes over happily thinking that her either her sister or her mother has been able to convince her father to let them join Egerton University. Her father has actually called her to tell her about her marriage to Oloisudori – the last thing Resian might expect. Her father is therefore taken by surprise when Resian mentions the matter about the university and as a result, he is unable to bring himself to broach the marriage topic. Other good examples of irony are on pgs. 182, 202, 203, 204 and 208.

Other aspects of style used include **repetition** for emphasis (as in the case of Egerton University), **wise sayings**, **satire** and **local language**. The sayings and local language especially emphasize the context and create verisimilitude. Oloisudori's character is satirized and so is that of the girls' parents.

WRITING YOUR ANSWERS IN LITERATURE

Literary writing is a well-thought-out process which you will have to cultivate yourself. Apart from practicing to write like others in the field, you need to adopt the right language, the correct diction and the appropriate styles; you need to know how to interpret questions, how to present answers and also do a lot of practice before the final exam so that planning, timing and other such impediments do not come in the way of performance. This section takes you through a careful planning and writing out of your essay, teaches you how to interpret context questions and shows you how to tell in no uncertain terms whether you have done what your examiner requires at every stage of the question by considering the marks awarded and how to earn them. This is done in five stages; interpreting questions, how to approach the context question, planning and writing out your essay, revising your essay and timing your essay.

I) Interpreting Questions.

It is important to seriously regard what certain question words mean because it is not uncommon to find a student go through the motions of answering a question but end up not doing so because the answer does not address the question. Here are the most common question words that you will find, especially in essay questions, with a considered opinion of what they require you to do. A sample question and the possible approach you might take to the question has also been given.

Analyze. Analyzing means examining *systematically* by *separating constituent parts* to see how they work together to form a unit. An analysis of a theme or a character, for example, will also involve an examination of the different aspects of that theme or character traits in order to show how they work together to form a writer's complete opinion of a subject or how the traits reflect a complete image of the character as shown in the particular text.

Sample Question: Analyze the theme of greed in H.R. ole Kulet's *Blossoms of the Savannah.*

Possible Approach: Go through the novel and examine how many greedy characters you can find. Examine the different types of greed and characters' motives, how they are presented and how they end up to form the author's opinion on the subject. Write out an essay showing these aspects of greed so as to show Ole Kulet's opinion of greed as a subject.

Compare. To compare, draw similarities between things. You might be asked to compare characters, treatment of themes or use of two aspects of style. For characters, discuss how they are treated; which one is more central than the other and what their roles are. For themes, discuss which is given more weight. For style, look at the way the two aspects of style are used; which one is more widely used/which one is more effectively used. Note that in some cases you may be required to compare and contrast.

Sample Question: Compare the treatment of male versus female characters in H.R. Ole Kulet's *Blossoms of the Savannah*.

Possible Approach: Draw two columns, one with male characters and the other with female characters. Go through the novel noting how each group is treated and suggesting the author's intention at every stage. Using the evidence collated, discuss how Ole Kulet treats characters according to gender while clearly showing their roles.

Contrast. To contrast is to draw out the outstanding differences between two things or people. To contrast two characters, show how they are unalike. To contrast two themes or aspects of style, show how differently they have been treated in the novel.

Sample Question: Contrast Resian and Taiyo in H.R. Ole Kulet's *Blossoms of the Savannah*.

Possible Approach: Examine the portrayal of the two characters in terms of traits and roles, how they begin and how they end, where they win and where they lose. Write an essay discussing this.

Describe. To describe is to draw a word picture which appeals to the sense of sight. An appeal to other senses such as smell, taste, hearing and touch helps too. In your description, ensure what you describe is 'seeable' and can be felt.

Sample Question: Describe how Ole Kaelo goes about trying to convince Resian to postpone her pursuit for university education.

Possible Approach: Go through Ole Kaelo and Resian's dialogue in chapter 14 noting arguments and counter-arguments relating to this question. Write an essay presenting this argument showing how far Ole Kaelo is deemed successful.

Discuss. To discuss, you need to convince your reader by examining an issue and shedding light on it, giving details while aiming at convincing your reader to see your point of view. This may require illustrations and explanations where you think your reader may be in the dark.

Sample Question: Discuss Ole Kulet's argument of culture through Ole Kaelo in H. R. Ole Kulet's *Blossoms of the Savannah*.

Possible Approach: List down points about positive and negative culture as seen through Ole Kaelo. Discuss reasons why Ole Kaelo engages in it and why you think this necessary/unnecessary or hypocritical on Ole Kaelo's part.

Evaluate. An evaluation is a judgment based on both your argument and evidence drawn from the text. It aims at persuading your reader to a certain point of view by using the evidence available as well as illustrations. It doesn't simply state an opinion.

Sample Question: Evaluate how convincing Minik ene Nkoitoi is as a character in H. R. Ole Kulet's *Blossoms of the Savannah*.

Possible Approach: Examine the character of Minik through behavior and opinion. Compare her with the everyday woman then write an essay that shows how similar or dissimilar she is.

Explain. To explain, make things clearer. Focus on issues and areas that are vague. This presupposes that the writer knows better than the reader and can guide the reader to see things more clearly.

Sample Question: Explain why Ole Kaelo finally decides to force Resian to marry Oloisudori in H. R. Ole Kulet's *Blossoms of the Savannah*.

Possible Approach: Follow Ole Kaelo's point of view of marriage through his reasoning from the beginning of the novel. Look at his arguments in chapter 14 then write an essay to make clear his thought processes and his decision.

Illustrate. To illustrate is to give good examples that support an idea. To support a character trait, give evidence that a character is what you claim s/he is. If you say, 'Taiyo is obedient,' anyone asking you to illustrate requires you to give evidence. Such evidence is an illustration.

Sample Question: Illustrating your answer, show whether you think Ole Kaelo greedy and materialistic or not.

Possible Approach: Collect evidence of Ole Kaelo's behavior in the novel especially towards material possessions. Examine his argument for marrying off Resian then say whether his life is driven by greed and materialism or not.

The strategies above should lead you to better interpret essay questions. Feel free to discuss other question words via our e-mail or our website.

ii) Dealing with the Context Question

Context usually refers to the area within which a word is used or a small part of the larger novel or play, short story and with questions set on it which test your understanding of both the short piece and its relationship to the text it is drawn from. 'Excerpt' may be used synonymously. Context questions may focus on plot, character, theme and style making them quite demanding. They require enough familiarity with the larger novel to answer analysis questions drawn from *any* part of the novel. You will be expected to properly place it within the rest of the story by saying what comes before and after it. This requires you to identify the *sub-conflict* in the excerpt, trace its origin *before* it and follow it to its end *after* (or sometimes within) the excerpt. The following excerpt from *Blossoms of the Savannah* should give you the idea.

Read the excerpt below and answer the questions which follow. (25 marks)

They also wanted to show him that they were young modern women who had their own pride, self-respect and **self-esteem.** They wanted him to know that they were not rudderless objects drifting in the sea without direction. They already had their aims and projections that could only be enhanced by the lofty ideas they held and the desire for higher learning at the university and career development. It was therefore **an insult to their intelligence, dignity** and integrity to think that mere material things such as the gifts he lavishly gave them would sway them from the goals they had already set for themselves.

"Since he seems to target me in his demonic designs," Resian said determinedly, "I shall try to face him bravely and tell him what I think of him, especially if he shows me his ill manners."

"Well, I don't know whether I would be able to face him alone," Taiyo said apprehensively. "He looked rapacious and I can't trust him if we are left alone with him in a room."

"The man is a monster. I fear him too," Resian said balefully. "It is only the desire to right things that gives me courage to face him. To speak the truth, when I think of the monster, I squirm in my shoes with fear!"

"What you should never accept, little sister," Taiyo told her sister emphatically, "is to be left alone in the house with the monster. However brave you are, you cannot be locked with a boar constrictor in a room and expect to survive."

"That I know, Taiyo-e-yeiyo," Resian answered **timidly**.

Questions

1. Place the excerpt in its immediate context. (4 marks)
2. With illustrations, identify one central theme in this excerpt. (3 marks)
3. Identify and explain one common aim the two girls in the excerpt have. (2 marks). How is this aim fulfilled in the end? (1 mark)
4. What 'material things' do the girls refer to or think about in the excerpt? Where do they come from and how do the girls treat them? (4 marks)
5. Who is the man referred to in the excerpt? (1 mark). Describe two ways in which this man displays 'ill manners' before this excerpt. (2 marks)
6. Identify and explain two images used in the excerpt and show their effectiveness. (4 marks)
7. Explain the meaning of the following words and phrases as used in context;

a. Self esteem
b. Insult to the intelligence
c. Dignity
d. Timidly (4 marks)

Possible Answers

1. As they wait for Oloisudori who is to visit their house that day, Taiyo

and Resian hatch up a plan to return the gifts he had given them on a previous visit. (1 mark). They are incensed by the fact that their father has already received a briefcase of money from Oloisudori which can only mean dowry for one of them. (1 mark). Oloisudori finally comes and the wrapped gifts are returned but Resian gets incensed when Oloisudori declares they are already married. (1 mark). She storms out of the home angrily and goes to confront her father. (1 mark)

2. This excerpt discusses early marriage/feminism. (1 mark). Resian learns that her father has already married her off and she is therefore supposed to postpone her going to the university. (1 mark) The author shows how women are objectified and their issues disregarded; Resian is married of without her consent; Oloisudori believes that he can buy the girls off by giving them gifts but the girls rebuff him by returning the gifts. (1 mark)
3. The common aim of the two girls is to join Egerton University. (1 mark). This aim is finally fulfilled when after being rescued by Minik ene Nkoitoi, both girls are given scholarships and Minik takes them to the university herself. (2 marks)
4. The material things the girls refer to are the silk materials of different colors for Taiyo and a pretty golden brooch and twelve lengths of different kinds of material for Resian. (2 mark). These gifts are given by Oloisudori and the girls decide to wrap them carefully and return them to Oloisudori. (2 marks)
5. The man referred to in the excerpt is Oloisudori. (1 mark). Before the excerpt, Oloisudori pays another visit to Kaelo's home. As her enters the house, he brushes against Resian's breasts; when he sits down, he ogles her lustfully hypnotizing and embarrassing her. (2 marks).
6. The images used include;

- The rudderless object drifting in the sea – this captures the purposelessness of life for many women who do not know what they want in life; the image contrasts the girls with such emphasizing their focused nature.

- Demonic designs emphasizes Oloisudori's wayward plans of trying to marry a girl young enough to be his daughter by force.

- Monster emphasizes the fact that Oloisudori's behavior is completely out of this world.

- Boa constrictor emphasizes the dangerous and treacherous nature of Oloisudori in that he cannot be trusted with a child.

Any 2 – identification 1 mark, effect 1 mark – total = 4 marks.

1. Meaning of words and phrases;

- Self-esteem – confidence in one's own worth and abilities

- Insult to the intelligence – affront/slur/abuse to their intellect/good thinking

- Dignity – honor and respect

- Timidly – shyly, fearfully, nervously (1 mark each – total=4 marks)

iii) Planning and Writing out a literary Essay

When you write essays, you need to plan your ideas and how to present them methodically. Worthy writers regard the opinion of the reader and write according to the reader's anticipation in order to make it easier for the reader to read. They also present points methodically since the easier it is for the reader to follow, the better the communication. As a student, you will also need to think like the examiner and decide at every point in your argument whether or not the examiner will follow and then make the necessary changes.

Plan to communicate in only six paragraphs. The essay you will write will be out of twenty marks; 2 will go to the introduction, 2 to the conclusion and 4 to language. Thus, the body of your essay will earn you 12 marks; that is 20 minus 8 (introduction, conclusion and language). For every point, you will be required to state the point, explain and illustrate and each point, each explanation and each illustration will earn you a single mark meaning any one well explained, well-illustrated point will earn you 3 marks. To earn twelve marks, you will need to present four well explained, well-illustrated points. Each of these points should be put in its own paragraph which means that to earn the twelve marks, you will need four well explained and well-illustrated points each in its own paragraph to form four paragraphs of the main body of your essay. If you add the introduction and the conclusion, then your essay should consist of only six paragraphs. Rather than do extra writing, refine what you have already written with better details, explanations and/or illustrations to any points which seem unclear. Extra points should only be written if the examiner requires you to do so, for example in a question such as; *Discuss **six** character traits of Parsimei Ole Kaelo.* Your planning and execution should follow a systematic formula that ensures that the examiner cannot deny you marks at any stage in your argument - you can even mark your own essay in your mind as you revise it and tell the margin within which your marks should lie.

Essay questions require you to confine yourself to 450 words. Do not to exceed the limit though under normal circumstances, a margin of five to ten words will be allowed on the plus or minus side. Whether or not this is required of you, learn to plan with this number of words in mind because often, it is the correct number to plan and execute for within the time you will be required to write your essay. The KCSE essay paper requires you to write three essays within two-and-a-half hours – a hundred and fifty minutes; that is fifty minutes for each essay. If you take five minutes to plan and five to revise, you only have forty minutes for writing each essay. The average student can only write a good paragraph within five to eight minutes, meaning that it would be quite unwise to plan for more than six paragraphs. See? Train yourself to plan, write and revise your essay with this number of words and the fifty minutes in mind so that your hand and your mind get used to this routine. If you plan with this in mind, then you will be required to write an average of 75 words in each of your six paragraphs, that is, 450 divided by six paragraphs. For a student with an average handwriting, this should be about one-and-a-half pages of a foolscap paper. In KCSE, this may be a little different because the margins of the answer sheet are slightly different. If you follow these directions truly, you will get used to the planning, execution and revision long before the exam comes; you won't have to worry about the time and the length of your essay.

In an exam situation, plan briefly on the question paper using key words to stand for what you intend to write so as to save time; plan fully within the first five minutes. Since you only have fifty minutes, five should be spent on planning and five for revision. No essay should ever be written without planning and likewise, none should ever be handed in without proper revision. Therefore, always plan with six paragraphs in mind, an average of 75 words to every paragraph and an average of six minutes to be spent writing each paragraph. In the following sample of a question, you can adopt the plan suggested in order to plan for and write six effective paragraphs.

Sample Question: Describe how Oloisudori goes about enticing the Kaelo family in an attempt to endear himself to them and marry Resian.

Possible Approach: Examine four good ways in which Oloisudori tries to entice the Kaelo family. Describe each in detail in its own chapter showing what Oloisudori intends at every stage. You can plan this way;

Paragraph 1 – introduction

Paragraph 2 – the first visit

Paragraph 3 – parents' invitation; house

Paragraph 4 – parents' invitation; the car

Paragraph 5 – second visit

Paragraph 6 – conclusion

To save time, use short words and phrases. Use key shortened words as long as you are sure you'll remember what you intended by them. Learn to use short word forms such as intro (introduction), Oloi (Oloisudori), JPmuat (Joseph Parmuat) xter (character) etc. This helps you to save time.

Against these words, give short details on how you'll develop the paragraph focusing on explanations and illustrations. Keep looking at the question to ensure you address it and fully satisfy its requirements. For this particular question, for example, the explanation and illustration should focus on how, at each stage, Oloisudori *tries to entice* by *engineering certain activities*. Note that the needs of each question may be unique. A question on character trait/stylistic devices requires you to illustrate while one on themes will require you to explain/make things clear. Decide the best way to fulfill the requirement of the question at hand as you plan. Let's first consider what a paragraph is.

What *is* a paragraph?

A paragraph is a group of sentences discussing **one idea**. That idea is captured in the **topic sentence** (usually, but not always, the first sentence of the paragraph). The topic sentence says what the paragraph is about while other sentences address or explain it. In the topic sentence, *I like reading*, the succeeding sentences must try to show *a number of things I do* which prove I *like* reading. They may proceed this way.

> *I like reading.* It really doesn't matter what time it is or where I am but I'll often find myself reading something. I make sure I read the morning papers before nine. Also, my travel bag always has the latest copy of *Reader's Digest* therefore I normally read it on my way to and from work. At the office, I'll always have some novel or other lying around because my job

> involves waiting and I often have long hours to myself doing nothing. I take advantage of this to read. I also like to take parked lunch at a bench in the public park and so I'll find myself reading a story alone as I go through lunch. Besides, there are several paperbacks next to my bedstead and I often find myself reading late into the night especially on weekends.

As you can see, all the sentences that succeed the topic sentence above point out a number of things about how I spend the day - they invariably show that reading is involved. Let us now consider the nature of an introductory paragraph of a literary essay.

A major variance of the initial paragraph above to an introductory paragraph of a literary essay is that while the one above is began by a **topic sentence**, the introductory paragraph of a literary essay contains a **theme statement** – a statement that captures what you intend to do in the whole essay. It also contains the title of the literary text of your argument and the name of the author. Underline the title of the text in handwritten work or italicize it in typewritten work. The author's name should be written in full – **H. R. O**le **K**ulet – using capitals for the initial letters of the name for it is a proper noun. For book titles, only key (content) words – nouns, verbs, adjectives and adverbs – should begin with capital letters e.g. **B**lossoms, **S**avannah etc. All others should be written in lower case unless they are the initial words of the title as in *A Doll's House* or *Blossoms **of** the Savannah*. Also, while the topic sentence is almost always the first sentence in a paragraph, a theme statement is almost always the last – at least in almost all well written essays.

Good theme statements often restate the question so as to ensure the salient elements of the question are retained and if you go ahead to plan and execute with the theme statement in mind, then you will be sure that your essay fully addresses the question - it isn't out of topic. For the essay question above, a good theme statement could be; **In H. R. Ole Kulet's *Blossoms of the Savannah*, Oloisudori also goes about**

enticing the Kaelo family so as to endear himself to them and marry Resian. Shorten it if need be, to get the number of words right.

An introductory paragraph serves to create rapport between us and the reader before we can formally communicate - human beings demand to be put in the right frame of mind before formal issues are introduced. Similarly, put the examiner in the right frame of mind before you discuss the issues at hand by beginning your essay in a general way. Do not jump in to talk about Oloisudori immediately. Use this leeway you've been given to capture the attention of the examiner in an interesting way. You can cleverly do this, by talking about how villains entice victims and alluding to another interesting book – like John Steinbeck's *The Pearl*. This way;

> Villains use a sweet tongue or flash their wealth about to lure their victims into their traps. In John Steinbeck's *The Pearl* for instance, the priest tells Kino about who he is named after to endear himself to Kino so that Kino can allow him to share in the profits of the pearl. Similarly, In H. R. Ole Kulet's *Blossoms of the Savannah*, Oloisudori tries to entice Kaelo's family so as to endear himself to them and marry Resian.

Remember to save words for there is neither time nor space to waste any. Note that the initial letters in the name of the author should be capitalized, the title of the text should be italicized in typewritten work or underlined in handwritten essays. Now let us focus again on the planning of the essay to see how this paragraph might have resulted from the student's initial planning.

Para 1 – introdn – villains, s/tongue, Steinbeck's priest, Blossoms t/state

Paragraph 2 – the first visit

Paragraph 3 – parents' invitation; house

Paragraph 4 – parents' invitation; the car

Paragraph 5 – second visit

Paragraph 6 – conclusion

Again, notice that these notes highlight the things the student will focus on once the writing begins. These key words will form the basis of sentences and will ensure that nothing is forgotten. There are no hard rules about how to proceed with the writing but you must ensure that the paragraph is clear and easily communicative for the examiner to follow your train of thought. The only other determinant might be the number of words. Be careful to communicate your idea fully in a paragraph of about 75 words to avoid being forced to use less words elsewhere and leave points hanging. Let us now consider the possible planning for the rest of the essay.

Para 1 – introdn – villains, Steinbeck's priest, Blossoms, t/state

Paragraph 2 – the first visit – d/shoe, suit, gold watch, bracelet, chain

Paragraph 3 – parents' invitation; house, cluster, view,

Paragraph 4 – parents' invitation; the car p/by, envy, decision

Paragraph 5 – second visit – limo. White, ornaments, sunshine

Paragraph 6 – conclusion – dress, planning, wealth-display

This student intends to focus on Oloisudori's first visit to the family in the second paragraph, focusing on his appearance and how it is meant to impress. He intends to talk about the worth of ornaments on Oloisudori's person. The first thing you need to remember is to use a connector to link the introduction to the second paragraph. Choose the connector carefully so as to link the introduction to the rest of the essay too. Suitable connectors to use here could be *first, to begin with, initially, firstly* etc. Next, take the keyword in the paragraph – visit – and using the connector, form the topic sentence to begin this paragraph. This way; *Firstly, Oloisudori's first visit is definitely meant to impress*. Next, use the other key words to form explanatory sentences to shape out the paragraph while explaining this topic sentence. This way;

> *Firstly, Oloisudori's first visit is definitely meant to impress.* He emerges from a high-sided vehicle and the first thing to be seen is the designer shoe. He wears a designer pin-striped business suit. He is also in a golden watch, a golden bracelet and a golden chain. All these are meant to show the family that he is not only rich but he can also afford to throw money about in luxuries.

Notice that you should use the key words to form the sentences that unravel the paragraph. This is done for as long as it takes to make the point clear remembering not to use too many words or time so as not to run out of both towards the conclusion. Now look at the planning above and write out the next three paragraphs in the same way *without looking at what is suggested below*. Once you've done this and you are confident about the way they turn out, the word limit as well as the apt diction, compare with what you've been given below. Remember to use appropriate connectors at the beginning of every paragraph. The connectors *second, another, secondly, next, also* can serve you for the third paragraph, *third, thirdly, also, next*, for the fourth and *last, lastly, finally, eventually* etc. for the fifth. If you use *next* somewhere, do not use it after that to avoid sounding redundant. Again, note that the connector to begin every successive paragraph might be determined by the one you used in the former paragraph. Now if you *have written* out your paragraphs, you can go ahead and compare with the following samples.

> Secondly, Oloisudori invites the couple to the house of wife number three. It is elegant with luxurious rooms and an elegant view of Lake Naivasha. Then they are taken to the expensive two-storied house Resian is supposed to occupy once married. It is just as elegant and luxurious. The floors are shiny and spacious while outside there is a swimming pool with a magnificent view of Lake Nakuru. The couple is awed.

> Thirdly, their trip from Oloisudori's home is meant to have a lasting effect. They are driven in a big strange vehicle which passers-by gape and dogs growl at. Ole Kaelo is so taken up in here that he looks at passers-by askance. Travelling through the rough roads makes the couple envious of Oloisudori the urbanite. This shows that the trip has the desired effect.
>
> Fourthly, Oloisudori's second visit crowns the lure of materialism. He arrives in a stately limousine, immaculately dressed as usual. He is in white trousers, white collarless shirt and white shoes. The golden ornaments are still in place but the absence of a suit is meant to emphasize these ornaments which glitter brilliantly in the sunshine. He is in a trimmed black moustache and carries an air of power with him. Again, the intention is unmistakable.

Now that is your complete essay except for the conclusion. To *conclude* is to wide up an argument – not to give any additional points but to tell your reader, '...that is all I had to say. This is where you and I part.' To do so, satisfy your reader by not leaving him/her hanging. This can happen if, when you attempt to conclude, you still sound like you are continuing your argument. Firstly, choose the right connector that warns your reader, '...now I'm about to go.' This way; *to conclude*, *in summary*, *as can be seen in the foregoing* etc. After this, use a statement that summarizes the points you've given to strike their relationship. For this particular essay, you can try something like *As can be deduced from the foregoing, Oloisudori does not just dress or ride a vehicle; whatever he does is meticulously planned in order to give a certain impression to his audience.* Then you can follow this with an explanation of what you mean before tying up with a striking statement about Oloisudori's character. You can try something like this.

> As can be deduced from the foregoing, Oloisudori does not just dress or ride a vehicle; whatever he does is meticulously planned in order to give a certain impression to his audience. He believes that his material possessions change the way people see him and therefore determine the way they are likely to deal with him afterwards. In the case of the Kaelo

family, all this display of wealth is meant to make the family want to share in Oloisudori's wealth should Resian marry him.

Now once through with this paragraph-by-paragraph planning and writing out of your essay, you should be rewarded with something like this;

Villains use a sweet tongue or flash their wealth about to lure their victims into their traps. In John Steinbeck's *The Pearl* for instance, the priest tells Kino about who he is named after to endear himself to Kino so that Kino can allow him to share in the profits of the pearl. Similarly, In H. R. Ole Kulet's *Blossoms of the Savannah*, Oloisudori tries to entice Kaelo's family so as to endear himself to them and marry Resian.

Firstly, Oloisudori's first visit is definitely meant to impress. He emerges from a high-sided vehicle and the first thing to be seen is the designer shoe. He wears a designer pin-striped business suit. He is also in a golden watch, a golden bracelet and a golden chain. All these are meant to show the family that he is not only rich but he can also afford to throw money about in luxuries.

Secondly, Oloisudori invites the couple to the house of wife number three. It is elegant with luxurious rooms and an elegant view of Lake Naivasha. Then they are taken to the expensive two-storied house Resian is supposed to occupy once married. It is just as elegant and luxurious. The floors are shiny and spacious while outside there is a swimming pool with a magnificent view of Lake Nakuru. The couple is awed.

Thirdly, their trip from Oloisudori's home is meant to have a lasting effect. They are driven in a big strange vehicle which passers-by gape and dogs growl at. Ole Kaelo is so taken up in here that he looks at passers-by askance. Travelling through the rough roads makes the couple envious of Oloisudori the urbanite. This shows that the trip has the desired effect.

Fourthly, Oloisudori's second visit crowns the lure of materialism. He arrives in a stately limousine, immaculately dressed as usual. He is in white trousers, white collarless shirt and white shoes. The golden ornaments are still in place but the absence of a suit is meant to emphasize these ornaments which glitter brilliantly in the sunshine. He is in a trimmed black moustache and carries an air of power with him. Again, the intention is unmistakable.

As can be deduced from the foregoing, Oloisudori does not just dress or ride a vehicle; whatever he does is meticulously planned in order to give a certain impression to his audience. He believes that his material possessions change the way people see him and therefore determine the way they are likely to deal with him afterwards. In the case of the Kaelo family, all this display of wealth is meant to make the family want to share in Oloisudori's wealth should Resian marry him. (447 words)

Now let us see what strategies you can use for the following essay questions from *Blossoms of the Savannah.*

Question 2.

'Young women in Kenya today can only succeed if they stand out from the crowd'. Using four outstanding traits of Minik ene Nkoitoi, discuss the truth of this statement.

Possible Approach: Choose four outstanding traits of Minik ene Nkoitoi. Discuss each of these traits in a paragraph of its own using illustrations of her portrayal in *Blossoms of the Savannah* to show that she stands out and inspires girls to do the same. This way;

Traits;

a) Well-educated b) Authoritative c) Determined d) caring/concerned

You can then plan in paragraph form to reflect the complete essay showing what will happen in each of the six paragraphs.

Introd – girls/society, indolent, complain, theme stat.

Para 2 – authoritative – command, to Resian, to Olois

Para 3 – education – Makerere, career,

Para 4 – Determined – abused, school, Taiyo, Olois,

Para 5 – caring/concerned– girls, Resian, Taiyo,

Concl – g/arguments no jobs, careers, need to be best, Ole Kulet

Planning here allows you to cover the question thoroughly by looking at it from all angles and by making sure it is fully addressed. It gives you enough material to cover all paragraphs – and the complete essay – so that, once the writing has begun, you can proceed without having to stop to consider what to say next. With good planning, you can write fully confident that there is time enough to finish and that all aspects of the question will be adequately addressed. You don't have to pause every now and then to consider whether or not you're still on track – this is in fact dangerous because it leads to unnecessary repetition and redundancy without the writer's knowledge. First, consider the theme statement - rephrase the question to form a good theme statement. Like this; **In *Blossoms of the Savannah*, Ole Kulet uses the character of Minik ene Nkoitoi to challenge such women to endeavor to stand out from the crowd**. The repetition of the key words of the question (underlined) in the theme statement ensures that the essay fully addresses the question. As you plan and write out the rest of the essay, ensure you faithfully follow what you set out to do in the theme statement – and in your initial plan - to avoid vagueness or straying away from the question.

> In today's competitive society, young women need to learn to do their best. If you look around, you will see many indolent women who sit back and complain about the lack of jobs and difficulties of the world while doing little about it. In his novel *Blossoms of the Savannah*, H R Ole Kulet uses the character of Minik ene Nkoitoi to challenge such women to endeavor to stand out from the crowd.

That's a fairly simple and straight forward introduction. As you write (both the paragraphs and the essay), keep the time and the number of words at the back of your mind so that you don't run wild and fail to get enough time for the ending. Now with this introduction, the rest of the essay can proceed this way.

> Firstly, Minik is authoritative. Her reputation and no nonsense character spreads far and wide leading her to be crowned Emakererei the wasp. She dares Ole Supeyo, for example, when she visits his home. Her authority is also seen in her command at Ntare-Naaju which is well-organized. Its size and functional nature says a lot more about her capability than anything else would – and so does her facing up to Oloisudori and his entourage.
>
> Minik is also well educated. In a community where girls are not only denied education but are married while still children, she manages to go all the way to Makerere University. This gives her an enviable job which inspires the likes of Resian and Taiyo. She also trains as a manager and her capability is seen both in the size of the farm she commands and in the supplicating nature of the men who work under her.
>
> Minik is similarly a determined young woman. Despite her young age in a community where elders are likened to Gods, she stands up to them where they are wrong. She is unrelenting in her campaign against FGM and early marriages. She argues with them as in the case of Ole Supeyo and where this fails, she uses force as can be seen in her rescuing Taiyo and rebuffing Oloisudori. This inspires all those working under her.
>
> However, Minik balances her commanding character with a caring and concerned heart. Resian is surprised that despite her command, she appears quite feminine. It is also out of her caring attitude that she rescues girls, takes them to school and ensures the likes of Nabaru understand just why she campaigns against FGM; it is not just a question of challenging men. The rite is backward, unhealthy and pointless.
>
> In conclusion therefore, it is apparent that many young women who complain about lack of jobs simply don't want to go the extra mile. They cover their laziness with excuses and this leads to their being taken advantage of by rich men in the society. Ole Kulet challenges such women that this can change – but they must be ready to wake up to the challenge and do a lot more by being the best they possibly can as demonstrated by Minik ene Nkoitoi.

(450 words)

Ensure too that you circumvent needless duplication particularly in the introduction and the conclusion. It may make your essay gloomy and drab. If you have to recap something as may become essential while concluding, choose synonyms prudently and make use of paraphrase.

3. "Female Genital Mutilation is a cruel excuse for upholding patriarchal authority". Using the experiences of Taiyo and Resian, discuss the verity of this observation.

Plan

Para 1 - Intrd – FGM, where, effect, theme s/ment

Para 2 – Ole Kaelo – emascul, b/failure, university,

Para 3 – Ole Kaelo - failure, education, hypocrisy, covetous

Para 4 – Oloisudori – chauvinism, ego, excuse, Supeyo-taming

Para 5 – parmuat/Nabaru – origin, no change, subservience

Para 6 – concl – pointless, personal reasons, hypocrisy, ego

Female Genital Mutilation is an obnoxious practice in many parts of Africa. While many people cannot trace its origin today, it has become apparent that it is often a health hazard that has a harrowing effect on its victims. It is often linked to mental trauma of those who undergo it, especially if they are forced to. In his novel, *Blossoms of the Savannah*, H R Ole Kulet shows that this custom is often an excuse for upholding patriarchal authority.

Firstly, Ole Kaelo hypocritically uses excuses to reassert his emasculated self when he is unable to face up to Oloisudori. He is taken advantage of by the latter and failing an alternative, he turns to exploit his daughters to reassert himself. To do so, the girls must get married as he says and FGM is a prerequisite to this. His behavior before this shows that he isn't an ardent believer in tradition thus his fall back on it is only an excuse.

Secondly, Ole Kaelo's business failure leaves him unable to educate his children. Unable to accept or explain this to the family, he decides to pretend that he is now an ardent believer in tradition which requires him to circumcise his girls and marry them off. His visit to Ole Supeyo and later to Oloisudori's home unmasks his covetous attitude and therefore, nobody believes his argument about his 'coming back to his people'.

Thirdly, Oloisudori himself shows that FGM and early child marriage are merely a sham for male chauvinism. His marrying many women only serves to bloat his ego; his using tradition to make this necessary, and his having them circumcised first is therefore a poor excuse for belief in tradition. Like Ole Supeyo, he believes that FGM is necessary to tame women a little before they are married, so they can be effectively ruled.

Lastly, both Parmuat and Nabaru show that FGM serves little purpose for the women themselves. Parmuat's explanation of its origin shows its original purpose serves no one today. Nabaru shows that those who undergo the rite are not any different from those who don't. Its use by the likes of Kaelo and Oloisudori only serves to make women feel subservient to them especially because it is men that insist on it.

In conclusion therefore, it is apparent that FGM plays no useful part in those societies that continue to uphold it. Its origin is itself suspect and in the novel, those men who insist on it are proven to have personal, hypocritical reasons for it. This way, Ole Kulet proves that FGM plays no useful part in society today and that only emasculated men will insist on it in an attempt to recapture their authority. (452 words)

iv) Revising Your Essay

Once you have written your essay, ensure that you have really done what you set out to do. No examiner will deny you marks for crossing out words and writing the correct ones above them, but you will lose marks if you don't correct your work. Often, the mind will be ahead of the hand – or the hand may be too tired to take some commands and the brain may lose its track. Go back to your work to ensure you did what you intended. It may not be as easy as it sounds. You may find that your mind gets this fixed idea about what you've written so that as much as you try to revise, you will tend to mentally correct wrong words and ideas by reading what you intended to write and not what you *actually* wrote. To correct this, you may need to do two things. First, learn to read your work objectively. This way, you may spot quite a number of the mistakes you might otherwise not have seen. Secondly, practice makes perfect. Write many essays and file them. Share them with other people. This way, your work will improve in a month more than it would have in a year.

Once you are confident with your essay writing skills, begin timing yourself. Take essays at random, plan and execute them and see how well you can answer them within the time required. Give them to your instructor or a friend and get their opinion. Revise it three times. During the first reading, examine the content against what you intended. In the second reading, check the language; examine word choice, sentence structure, phrases, idioms and metaphors. In the third reading, check the grammar. Examine the punctuation, spelling, grammar and capitalization. Rewrite take-away essays if you have to.

v) Timing Your Essay

One *last* thing. Timing the planning and the writing of your essay is a crucial skill to learn and practice. If you are writing essays for paper 3 in KCSE, the time allowed is two-and-a-half hours or a hundred and fifty minutes for three essays. This translates into fifty minutes for every essay. Plan in five minutes, then write every paragraph in five to six minutes. This should take up a maximum of forty one minutes leaving you a comfortable nine minutes to revise your work. This also ensures that should you make a mistake somewhere, you will have enough time to consider the mistake and decide what to do. This may not be so practical for the second and the third essay for you will continue to get tired as you write. Again, there are no hard rules about this. Learn to practice early so that you aren't caught off guard.

A CATALOGUE OF LITERARY TERMS

The following is a list of literary terms that relate to the novel. Read and comprehend them. They will help you follow literary arguments and write good essays yourself. Read extensively to see other literary terms not in this list, particularly those that relate to drama and poetry.

ALLUSION is a reference to a person, place or thing that is commonly understood from literature, religion, history, mythology, politics, sports or even another area known to many people. *The lady with the lamp*, for example, alludes to the world's most celebrated nurse, Florence Nightingale. *A Robinson Crusoe* can only allude to Daniel Defoe's stranded hero in the book by the same name. Anyone calling you this suggests you are really innovative.

ATMOSPHERE is the general mood in a literary text such as a novel or a part of it. It is often captured in a single adjective such as miserable, pessimistic, poignant, frightening, daunting etc. Atmosphere is often created through word choice and the images painted by this diction.

CHARACTER A character is a person, animal and sometimes an inanimate being that features in a literary text. In ordinary works of literature, characters are people like us who live and die in a world like our own. In myths and legends, characters may be animals, gods, or even physical features such as rivers and mountains. In a novel, characters are built through what they say or do. They may also be built through what we learn of them through other characters. Characters who change between the time we meet them and the time we leave them are **dynamic**. Those that don't are **static**. A **flat** character is one with one or two traits that don't change. A **round** one has many complex traits which develop and change within the context of the story. Nabaru is a dynamic character while Milanoi is largely static.

CHARACTERIZATION is the process of creation of characters. In a novel, we learn about characters mostly as a result of direct description by the narrator, through the comments made about them by others and through how the characters themselves talk and behave.

CLIMAX The point at which events, emotions and feelings are at their most intense. This could be the point at which the leading character is facing the height of a crisis. After this, the action can only decline because the turn of events, and sometimes how the story will end has already been determined. Resian's escape to Minik is the climax of *Blossoms of the Savannah*.

COMEDY This is a novel or a part of a novel that is largely hilarious and makes the audience laugh. Many comedies use hyperbole to blow characters and their conditions out of proportion so as to make them humorous. Humor is created in Oloisudori's escape to emphasize his cowardice.

COMPARISON This is the attempt to compare two literary pieces or characters or the treatment of certain literary aspects such as themes or styles in a literary text. A comparison may involve balancing the likes and the dislikes. At other times, a base for this comparison such as negative or positive, character, style etc. may be given.

CONFLICT This is a clash between two emotions or forces or even characters in a literary text. When it occurs within a character, e.g. when a character struggles to keep from crying, it is **internal**. When it occurs between two forces or characters such as the one between the rich and the poor, an individual and another, it is **external**.

CONNOTATION is a meaning drawn from what we associate a word with rather than what it means, that is, its associative meaning, not its literal one. The word 'mother' literally means she who gives birth to another. Its associative or connotative meaning however is one who nurtures another whether they gave birth to them or not. Literary texts use connotation widely to build characters that aren't obvious and sometimes to underscore themes.

CONTEXT means the area within which a word or a phrase is used; its general locality. It may also refer to a particular area of interest e. g an *excerpt* picked from a larger piece of writing. Context is often crucial in unraveling meanings of unfamiliar words, even words in a foreign language. In the sentence,

> The *Lobotose* gave a loud whine as it awkwardly turned slowly at the roundabout then tried to slide between two buses into a parking lot grazing their sides with a jarring noise.

We can tell that the nonsense word *Lobotose* refers to a large machine such as a combine harvester, ground leveler or tank. The meaning of this word can be inferred from the context, that is, the way it is used within the sentence. Since you cannot rely on a dictionary all the time, you must teach yourself to infer the meaning of words from their context.

CONTRAST This refers to an obvious difference between two or more things, characters or even objects. In Literature, it may refer to a novelist's juxtaposition of two things or characters. In *Blossoms of the Savannah,* it may refer to the difference in the character of Resian and Taiyo.

CROSS PURPOSE in a novel refers to a dialogue where characters talk at one another rather than to one another. This happens when characters follow varying trains of thought so that they appear to be talking to each other but their speech shows disjointedness because each character is thinking of different things.

DESCRIPTION This is a speech that appeals to the senses of sight, smell, touch, taste and/or hearing so as to make the audience 'see' the character, place or event so described. Description aims at creating mental pictures by engaging these senses. In a novel, this usually occurs through narration.

DIALECT A dialect is a way of talking that is typical of a certain geographical region or a specific group of people especially as seen as a part of a larger group. It is an offshoot of another more standard language which may be considered its mother language. A dialect signals a character's regional location and sometimes social and economic standing.

DIALOGUE This is speech between characters. In novels, what characters say is put in opening and closing speech marks with a phrase after it which shows how it is said, (*shaking his head*, *smiling*, *whispering* etc.) Dialogue is one of the major ways of character revelation because characters make themselves what they become from what they say as opposed to our being told by others what they are. A **monologue** or **soliloquy** is an instance where a character speaks alone or to him/herself.

DICTION This is the word choice chosen by a novelist or a speaker. Diction is important because at the back of our minds, we remember that a writer or speaker had a choice to use different words. Therefore, a certain type of diction is seen as a deliberate choice for a specific purpose. Diction may be used to differentiate characters' age, economic class or social standing. It is therefore crucial in character formation. .

ESSAY This is a short piece of non-fiction prose. Essays may be formal or informal but the ones you will be expected to write in Literature are formal. They will require you to write on a certain topic giving your opinion and illustrating what you say to convince your reader.

EXAGGERATION This refers to taking the action further than what is believable or expected. In novels, this often serves to ridicule characters and their actions, sometimes with comic effect. In *Blossoms of the savannah*, for example, Oloisudori's behavior is exaggerated to satirize him.

FICTION This refers to an imaginary account as opposed to a factual one. Many fictional accounts are created from what has been observed but characters and details are changed to suit a writer's specific purpose.

FIGURE OF SPEECH This is a word or phrase which describes something in terms of something else so that it cannot be taken literally. It involves an imaginative likening of two things which are ordinarily unlike. The most common figures of speech are;

I) **simile** – a direct comparison of one thing with another which uses the comparative words 'like', 'than', 'as', or 'resembles' e.g. *In the evening half-light, the mountain looked* **like** *an ogre with its shoulders hunched*, or *From where I stood, Amy looked taller* **than** *she really was*, or *The early morning sky was* **as** *clear* **as** *a mountain spring* or *Seen through the bead curtain, Amy* **resembled** *a bronze Roman statue.*

II) **Metaphor** – it is an indirect comparison that says something *is* something else rather than say it *looks* like it. For example, *Angered by her team, Amy was a lioness that had lost its cubs* or *With her right hand raised, Amy was the queen awarding a medal of honor.*

III) **Personification** – a comparison of the behavior of a non-living being to that of the living e.g. *The giant rock sulked dreamily in the sweltering heat.*

FLASHBACK This is a pause in the current action of the plot in order to look back at an event(s) that happened before now. This often happens when the past event(s) is deemed crucial in the understanding of the current one.

FOIL A foil is a character whose purpose is to contrast another so that the other is better perceived. Taiyo in *Blossoms of the Savannah* can be seen as a foil to Resian in her lack of assertiveness as opposed to her sister's rebellious nature.

FORESHADOWING (Adumbrating) The opposite of flashback, this is a pause in the current narrative in the plot in order to consider events that will happen later in a character's life or things a character will do later in the narrative. A novelist may describe an action or an object in a way that it points to its own significance later in the narrative. Ole Supeyo's description of Oloisudori foreshadows the latter's taking advantage of Ole Kaelo in demanding to marry his daughter.

IMAGERY This refers to the use of language or words that appeal to the senses, especially the sense of sight so as to make it possible for an audience to see what is being described. Good imagery paints a word picture that is recognizable to the audience. The most basic way of doing this is by using apt similes and metaphors but a word picture can also be drawn by a description that covers several lines or even a paragraph. It may also appeal to other senses apart from sight.

INFERENCE An inference (reading between the lines) is a conclusion that is made by putting two and two together rather than considering individual words or incidences. Inference is often made from educated guesses that point to possibilities rather than considering specific facts. If a number of things get lost in your class over a period of time every time you go for P.E, then by coincidence it happens that one of you happens to be absent from the lesson on those occasions, then the rest of the class can easily infer that the individual is the thief. We can easily infer Ole Kaelo's reason of marrying off Resian by considering his failure in business and his intimidation by Oloisudori.

IRONY refers to a seeming discrepancy between what seems to be and what really is. Often, we understand irony by seeing the contradiction between what is said and what is meant, what appears to be and what really is. **Verbal irony** is a case where what is said is the direct opposite of what is meant. If your Mathematics teacher tells you, 'How now, my newfound genius,' when you've scored twelve per cent, then you know s/he is being ironical. **Litotes** is a special case of verbal irony which involves the use of the negative 'not' with an adjective to emphasize its opposite. When somebody says, 'Madam was not a little upset,' we know they mean, 'Madam was very furious.' Similarly, when somebody says, 'It won't be an easy journey,' we know they mean that the journey will be difficult – very difficult. **Situational irony** refers to a case where what happens is the opposite of what we expected would happen. If your friend invites you to a strange neighborhood for a birthday party where you end up lost, mugged, penniless and rained on, then your situation is ironical; rather than party yourself to boot as you expected, you end up a lot worse than you were initially. **Dramatic irony** refers to a case where the reader has more information about what is going on than the character(s); for example, we pity Resian more because we know that her parents have already planned to marry her off behind her back while she is only forced to use clues such as the briefcase to try and tell what is going on.

LEGEND A legend is a character who makes such an impact that when s/he leaves, s/he is remembered long afterwards. A living legend is one whose impact is felt in his/her own life time.

METAPHOR This is an indirect comparison of one thing with another where the being (the thing being used to compare) and the referent (the thing referred to) are said to be one another, rather than being said to look like one another. When we say someone has a heart of gold, we do not mean that their hearts are precious metals; we mean that they are kind; we mean that they are easily moved by the circumstances of other individuals. As noted above, metaphors avoid direct words of comparison such as *as*, *like*, *than* and *resembles*. Instead, they interweave the being with the referent both of which are seen in terms of one another. A writer may use several elements of the being to compare it with the referent. For example, a writer can use an ogre's eating habit, its size, its looks, its fantastic nature and its cannibal character to compare it with a man's greed, physique, outrageousness and treachery. This kind of metaphor uses several aspects of the being to bring the referent to focus. It is referred to as an **extended metaphor**.

MOTIF This refers to a recurring idea that points to its own significance. It could be a repeated event that points to the fact that it should not be taken lightly. For many motifs, the repeated idea or event often leads to the same thing which suggests that what it leads to might be more significant than the idea or the event itself. For example, a number of characters may take significant journeys at different times within the narrative. Every time a journey happens, the lives of the individuals change significantly. This way, the writer might suggest the importance of journeys in people's lives, like say, the idea that journeys usually lead to rejuvenation and change in people's lives. Journey in this case becomes a motif. A motif can be introduced by different ideas or sometimes symbols. Recurring smashed windows together with adultery and runaway children such as teenagers, when seen together may suggest family disintegration. Dreams in *Blossoms of the Savannah* are a motif.

MOTIVATION is the reason that drives a character's behavior. Since a character can act out of longing, raw feeling, encouragement etc., motivation becomes crucial in our attempts to understand the true nature of a character. Ole Kaelo's insistence on culture and tradition may seem baffling until we understand his failure in business and the nature of his benefactor, Oloisudori.

NARRATION refers to telling a story through a third person narrator, often the omniscient narrator as opposed to dialogue which uses the first person point of view. Narration is crucial in covering ground in a story and in giving alternative points of view from those of characters. This makes a story rich and multi-faceted. A narration of events exposes the conflict and moves the action forward through the main stages of the story, often identified as **exposition**, **complications**, **climax** and **resolution**.

NOVEL This is a work of fiction which tells a story through characters and events created by the writer (who is called a novelist). Novels use imaginary events imagined by the novelist or sometimes mix the real and the unreal. A novel will usually have over 40 000 words - shorter than this will be referred to as a novella, shorter than 15 000 words, a short story. A novel will also have many complex characters with many extensive situations. It will therefore discuss many themes, though there will always be one or two outstanding ones.

PLOT is the series of connected incidents that make up a story. A properly worked out plot should have an identifiable *beginning* (often referred to as the *doormat* or *exposition*) where a certain situation is exposed. After this *introduction*, events follow each other in a **cause and effect** way to lead to *complications*. This means that the events do not follow the predictable or expected pattern giving room for the narrative to continue. A good complication leads to *rising action*, which in itself leads to a *climax*. The climax is followed by *falling action* or *denouement* which should lead logically to a conclusion.

PROTAGONIST This is the leading character in a work of literature such as a novel. S/he is the one who is involved in the main conflict. If there happens to be another major character against who the protagonist is pitted, then that is the **antagonist**. The protagonist is often the hero or the leading character with whom we identify. Such characters usually run the length of the narrative. In *Blossoms of the Savannah,* Resian can easily be identified as the protagonist for she embodies the leading theme. Oloisudori is the antagonist.

PUN is a play on words, often from the way they sound and sometimes from what they mean. A **homophonic** pun is one that plays on two words which sound the same. E.g. *The king was worried about his receding heir line.* A pun on 'hair' and 'heir' – and of course with a mispronunciation of the latter which adds to the fun of the pun. A **homographic** pun plays on the two meanings of a word. E.g. *When Nancy sits there all day with her needle and thread, she turns quite a sewer.* Meaning: *She sweats and smells like a conduit for water or sewage* or *She becomes so practiced that she is an expert sewer* (one who sews with needle and thread).

SETTING refers to the time and place context within which the action in the story happens. The realism of a story will depend on how much the novelist is able to make us feel that we live in a certain historical time and place. An audience needs to take this into account so as to properly judge characters and to perceive themes the way they are intended and also to be able to pass judgment on the quality of work that a novelist comes up with.

SIMILE A direct likening or comparison of one thing with another using the words *as*, *like*, *than* or *resembles*. For example, *Amy's dress was* **as** *yellow* **as** *a blossoming daffodil* or *Amy sang* **like** *a twenty-first century Ruby Green* or *Amy is brighter* **than** *her sister* or *Amy* **resembles** *her aunt.*

STYLE is the manner in which a novelist uses or handles language to achieve a certain end. It may also refer to the way the novelist uses literary aspects, or devices of style to shape a narrative e.g. use of images, symbolism etc. It also involves the diction or choice of words as well as the sentence structure and the aim with which the author uses this and how far success is met.

SUSPENSE is the handling of the plot to create tension and anxiety that keeps the reader glued to the text. If you should find yourself eagerly wondering what will happen next, it means the story you are dealing with is full of suspense. If the narrative is the food that the writer serves the reader, then suspense is the spice which makes one writer's dish different from another's.

SYMBOL A symbol is a person, thing, place or event that has two meanings; it has its own meaning and also represents something wider than itself. A symbol could be something that we use daily and which we all agree represents something else, the way a star and a crescent moon represent Islam, a cross Christianity or a flag an independent nation, or it could be something personal built within a novel and made to represent something wider than itself.

THEME is the main idea(s) discussed in a text. Theme is separate from subject. Most subjects are potentially controversial ideas which we live with and about which people have an opinion. Religion, marriage, betrayal, disillusionment and culture are famous subjects in literature. Subjects such as pets, diet, celibacy and alcoholism are more personal. The opinions we have about these subjects are what is called themes. While it is easy to capture a subject in a word, a theme can only be put in a statement because it represents one's opinion about a certain subject. About religion, one could say, 'Religion is the opium of the poor.' This is an opinion; it is therefore a theme. Of marriage one could say, 'Marriage is the tomb of love.' This is a debatable, controversial opinion; it is a theme. In a work of Literature with the span of a novel, there will be many subjects discussed as well as many opinions expressed about each subject. In discussing a theme, identify a subject, gather all available information on it with reasons and enough illustrations. Discuss these opinions systematically giving enough illustrations at every stage. The totality of what you come up with can be said to be the treatment of that theme in that text.

TRAGEDY is a literary piece in which the hero loses. Tragedies discuss serious issues about which the hero is the leading light and about which the audience expects a good and noble hero/heroine to win or conquer the situations facing him/her but s/he doesn't, often resulting in abject defeat, even death. Tragedies leave audiences deflated after identifying with a hero or heroine who fails, often due to a tragic error in their character or conditions beyond their control.

UNDERSTATEMENT The contrast of exaggeration, an understatement says less than it should often with an ironic turn. A leader who says 'It was not easy' after a war in which he loses all his soldiers, really means 'It was very difficult.' The choice of words may be intentionally intended to stress or highlight the seriousness of the situation thus stressing it. This is called understatement.

VILLAIN refers to the leading hateful character or the bad guy in a literary work. Often, this is the character through who the audience is warned against bad behavior for they suffer the consequences of bad choices. The villain is often the opponent of the hero or sometimes (but not always) the antagonist. A villain is the leading character who is devoted to evil or wickedness in a literary text. In *Blossoms of the savannah,* Oloisudori is largely the villain.

Did you love *H R ole Kulet's Blossoms of the Savannah: A Complete Guide*? Then you should read *Margaret Ogola The River and the Source: A Complete Guide*[1] by Jorges P. Lopez!

[2]

The study of the modern African novel has been quite a challenge both at the high school and at the university level. This is especially so for novels that address traditional tenets of the African society. These novels, however, form a good corpus as a basis for comparative literature, especially looking at the African novel as compared to its European or the American counterpart. Still, the odinary critic is used to earlier African writers including Ngugi, Achebe, Soyinka and the rest. Margaret Ogola presents a challenging novel in The River and the Source because it examines the modern African society. This critical book of this novel affords the reader all the necessary angles from

1. https://books2read.com/u/3kD92O

2. https://books2read.com/u/3kD92O

which this novel can be seen including Plot, Character, Themes and Elements of Style. It goes further to examine common ways of examining the novel by giving excerpt and essay questions and explaining in detail how such questions should be approached. The book focuses on the national exam in Kenya - the Kenya Certificate of Secondary Examination through which candidates matriculate and qualify for entry to the university. This, however, should give a good insight to any candidate worldwide regardless of the examination they are supposed to sit for. The book looks at the division of time as well as thinking how to earn marks and ensuring the candidate ganers as much as possible of what is given. These explanations will allow the candidate of a different examination to adjust depending on the time allowed and the marks given for questions in that particular examination. This makes this book applicable to the student of the novel - and the African novel in particular - anywhere in the world.

About the Author

Jorges P. Lopez has been teaching Literature in high schools in Kenya and Communication at The Cooperative University in Nairobi. He has been writing Literary Criticism for more than fifteen years and fiction for just over ten years. He has contributed significantly to the perspective of teaching English as a Second Language in high school and to Communication Skills at the college level. He has developed humorous novellas in the *Jimmy Karda Diaries Series* for ages 9 to 13 which make it easier for learners of English to learn the language and the *St. Maryan Seven Series* for ages 13 to 16 which challenge them to improve spoken and written language. His interests in writing also spill into Poetry, Drama and Literary Fiction. He has written literary criticism books on Henrik Ibsen, Margaret Ogola, Bertolt Brecht, John Steinbeck, John Lara, Adipo Sidang' and many others.

www.ingramcontent.com/pod-product-compliance
Lightning Source LLC
LaVergne TN
LVHW091057150826
845673LV00002B/621

* 9 7 9 8 2 2 3 6 2 6 6 3 3 *